MW01126441

Table of Contents

Introduction... 6

Breakfast Recipes.. 7

Breakfast Pizza...7

Donuts..7

Crepes...8

Waffles..8

Herbed Eggs..9

No at meal..9

Chia Pudding...10

Granola..10

Yogurt Bowl..11

Morning Coffee Shake..11

Tofu Scramble..12

Zucchini Tots...12

Fragrant Smoothie..13

Breakfast Bagels..13

Almond Scramble..14

Vanilla Sticks...14

Pancakes...15

Green Frittata...15

Breakfast Bread...16

Breakfast Chocolate Balls...16

Dill Mushroom Hats..17

Coconut Porridge..17

Keto Casserole...18

Cup Muffin..18

Spinach Muffin 19

Lunch Recipes..**20**

Cauliflower Hash Brown Bowl..20

Baked Asparagus with Eggs 20

Broccoli Fritters...21

Green Beans Salad 21

Risotto..22

Eggplant Rolls...22

Zucchini Gratin...23

Zucchini Boats..23

Eggplant Gratin 24

Greek Salad 24

Portobello Mushrooms...25

Avocado Eggs 25

Kale Soup 26

Spinach Pie...26

Tofu Wraps...27

Bok Choy Salad...27

Avocado Pie 28

Turnip Gratin..28

Gnocchi..29

Spinach Soup..29

Eggplant Pizza 30

Falafel 30

Egg Salad..31

Quesadillas...31

Cheese Rolls 32

Side Dishes **33**

Mashed Cauliflower 33

Fragrant Cauliflower Steaks...33

Fried Cheese..34

Cabbage Salad...34

Hummus 35

Roasted Halloumi..35

Roasted Cabbage 36

Deviled Eggs 36

Fried Broccoli 37

Brussel Sprouts with Nuts 37

Zucchini Pasta...38

Shirataki Noodles 38

Low Carb Baked Vegetables 39

Rutabaga Swirls 39

Fettuccine 40

French Fries...40

Broccoli Fritters..41

Spinach in Cream..41

Dill Radish...42

Curry Rice 42

Garlic Artichokes 43

Turnip Slaw...43

Sauteed Cabbage...44

Spiced Rutabaga 45

Swiss Chard 45

Main Dishes... **46**

Enchiladas 46

Keto Satay...46

Zucchini Tart...47

Pierogi 47

Creamed Leek...48

Mint Fritters 48

Tikka Masala 49

Lasagna...49

Casserole 50

Quiche 50

Nachos..51

Stuffed Zucchini Pancakes..51

Artichoke Peppers 52

Nut Salad..52

Caprese...53

Eggplant Salad 53

Tricolore Salad 54

"Potato" Salad...54

Florentine 55

Rutabaga Wedges 55

Fried Eggplants...56

Crunchy Asparagus Sticks 56

Caesar 57

Almond Cheese...57

Cabbage Fritters..58

Desserts.. 59

Vegan Chocolate Bars...59

Brown Fat Bombs..59

Nut Fudge 60

Mug Cake 60

Cocoa Ice Cream 61

Almond Fat Bombs 61

Brownies 62

Cheesecake 62

Chocolate Shots 63

Macaroons 63

Zucchini Bars 64

Coconut Cookies 64

Red Velvet Muffins 65

Gingerbread Muffins 65

Eggnog 66

Chocolate Pumpkins 66

Almond Cupcakes 67

Dulce De Leche 67

Carrot Cakes 68

Chocolate Pie 68

Keto Cookies 69

Mousse 69

Delicious Sweet Shake 70

Avocado Pops 70

Caramel 71

Conclusion **72**

Recipe Index **73**

Introduction

The trend of vegetarian is mis traced during the last few years. People all over the world become vegetarians. One of them avoid animal products with respect to nature and the environment in general, another one believes that vegetarianism is healthier in comparison with other types of diets. However, there are cases when people should restrict the consumption of animal products because of health problems such as diabetes or any other diseases which cause a need for controlling the level of sugar in the blood.

The main condition for the Keto diet is restrictions of carbs and consuming of high protein food. Is it possible to follow it if you are a vegetarian? You can be calm, vegetarian Keto diet is possible to follow! Nevertheless, it is worth noting that the risk of protein, mineral, and vitamin deficient is higher.

There are four main types of vegetariants. Let's consider each of them in a more detailed way. Vegans avoid almost all animal products including dairy products, eggs, meat, poultry, and seafood. In some cases, even honey can be restricted.

Lacto vegetarians have fewer restrictions. During this diet, you should avoid eggs, any type of meat, poultry,and seafood. Nevertheless, it is allowed to consume dairy products. Indian vegetarians follow this type of diet.

During Lactoovo vegetarian diet you can eat dairy product and eggs but avoid meat, poultry, and seafood. This is the most popular way of vegetarianism in the US and Europe. The last type is the pescatarians. It is possible to consider this diet as a semi-vegetarian. You can allow to eat dairy products, eggs, and even seafood but restrict meat and poultry. Pestacarians have the lowest level of risk in nutrient deficiencies. Theoretically, the Keto diet can be incorporated almost in every vegetarian day plan. Due to the type of diet the range of meals can be changed. Nevertheless, practically restriction of almost all proteins doesn't work very well. Animal proteins are rich in vital amino acids for maintaining the healthy state of the body. The greens can only contain and complement some of them. Depends on your Keto meal plan the consumption of net carbs can be up to 20 net carbs per day. In this cookbook, you will find the recipes for every type of vegetarians. Always remember that it is important to take the issue of nutrition and the choice of a meal plan. If you are a vegetarian and want to follow Keto lifestyle it is recommended to consult a doctor and make the full body examination. The self-prescribed diet can lead to irreversible effects in your body.

Breakfast Recipes

Breakfast Pizza

Prep time: *10 minutes* | *Cooking time:* *15 minutes* | *Servings:* 4

Ingredients:

- 1 cup cauliflower, shredded
- 3 tablespoon almond flour
- ¼ teaspoon salt
- 2 eggs, beaten
- 1 cup spinach, chopped
- 1 oz Parmesan

Directions:

Whisk the eggs and combine them together with almond flour, salt, and shredded cauliflower. Stir the mixture until smooth. Line the pizza mold with the baking paper and transfer the cauliflower dough inside it. Flatten the cauliflower crust gently. Place the spinach over the pizza crust. Grate the cheese and sprinkle the spinach. Preheat the oven to 365F. Put the pizza in the oven and cook for 15 minutes or until cooked.

Nutrition value/serving: calories 182, fat 14.3, fiber 3.1, carbs 6.5, protein 10.3

Donuts

Prep time: 15 minutes | *Cooking time: 25 minutes* | *Servings: 4*

Ingredients:

- 1 egg, beaten
- 1 cup almond flour
- 1 teaspoon vanilla extract
- 2 tablespoon butter
- 1 teaspoon baking powder
- 1 tablespoon ground cinnamon
- 3 tablespoon swerve

Directions:

Make the donut dough: mix up together beaten egg, almond flour, vanilla extract, butter, and baking powder. Knead the soft and non-sticky dough. Let it rest for 10 minutes. Meanwhile, preheat oven to 365F. Line the tray with the parchment. Roll up the dough and make the donuts with the help of the cutter. Transfer the donuts on the tray and put in the oven. Cook the donuts for 25 minutes or until light brown. Meanwhile, mix up together swerve and ground cinnamon. Coat the hot cooked donuts in the cinnamon mixture.

Nutrition value/serving: calories 119, fat 10.4, fiber 1.7, carbs 5.2, protein 3

Crepes

Prep time: 10 minutes | *Cooking time: 10 minutes* | *Servings: 7*

Ingredients:
- 1 cup coconut flour
- 1/3 cup almond milk
- 1 teaspoon swerve
- 1 teaspoon vanilla extract
- 1 egg, beaten
- 2 tablespoon flax meal

Directions:
Mix up together all the ingredients in the mixing bowl. Whisk the mixture until homogenous and smooth. The mixture should have sour cream texture. Preheat the non-stick pan. Ladle the 1 ladle of the crepe mixture in the pan. Cook every crepe for 1 minute from each side over the medium-high heat.

Nutrition value/serving: calories 115, fat 5.8, fiber 7.7, carbs 13.1, protein 3.8

Waffles

Prep time: 8 minutes | *Cooking time: 10 minutes* | *Servings: 4*

Ingredients:
- 3 egg whites
- 4 tablespoon almond flour
- 1 tablespoon swerve
- ½ teaspoon baking powder
- 1 teaspoon vanilla extract
- 2 teaspoon butter
- 1 tablespoon heavy cream

Directions:
Whisk the egg whites until soft peaks. Then add almond flour, swerve, baking powder, vanilla extract, and heavy cream. Stir the mixture well. Melt the butter and add in the batter. Stir it well until smooth. Preheat the waffle maker and pour the mixture inside it. Cook the waffles according to the directions of waffle maker manufacturer or until they are golden brown.

Nutrition value/serving: calories 208, fat 17.3, fiber 3, carbs 7.2, protein 8.8

Herbed Eggs

Prep time: 10 minutes | Cooking time: 5 minutes | Servings: 4

Ingredients:

- 8 eggs
- 1 tablespoon butter
- 1 teaspoon olive oil
- 1 teaspoon chili flakes
- 1 teaspoon dried oregano
- ½ teaspoon salt
- 1 teaspoon garlic powder

Directions:

Boil the eggs in the saucepan for 5 minutes. Meanwhile, melt the butter and combine it together with olive oil. Add chili flakes, dried oregano, salt, and garlic powder. Whisk the mixture. When the eggs are cooked – chill them in the ice water and peel. Then place the eggs in the serving plates and sprinkle with the herbed buttermixture.

Nutrition value/serving: calories 165, fat 12.9, fiber 0.2, carbs 1.5, protein 11.3

No at meal

Prep time: 5 minutes | Cooking time: 2.5 minutes | Servings: 3

Ingredients:

- 4 tablespoon coconut shred
- 2 tablespoon chia seeds
- 2 tablespoon hemp seeds
- 1 tablespoon almond flour
- 1 teaspoon vanilla extract
- 1 tablespoon swerve
- 1 cup almond milk
- 1 tablespoon almonds, crushed

Directions:

Take the glass bowl and combine together all the ingredients in it. Stir until homogenous. Cook the no at meal in the microwave oven for 2 minutes. Then stir the meal and cook it for 30 seconds more. Chill the no at meal until warm.

Nutrition value/serving: calories 362, fat 33.1, fiber 6.7, carbs 12.6, protein 8.1

Chia Pudding

Prep time: 8 minutes | Cooking time: 5 hours | Servings: 2

Ingredients:
- ½ cup almond milk
- 4 teaspoon chia seeds
- 1 teaspoon vanilla extract
- 1 tablespoon swerve
- 1 oz blackberries

Directions:
In the food processor blend together almond milk, vanilla extract, swerve, and blackberries. When the mixture is smooth – pour it in the serving glasses. Add chia seeds and stir gently. Transfer the glasses in the fridge and let them rest for 5 hours. Stir the pudding well before serving.

Nutrition value/serving: calories 256, fat 20.9, fiber 9.4, carbs 14.9, protein 5.1

Granola

Prep time: 10 minutes | Cooking time: 15 minutes | Servings: 2

Ingredients:
- 2 tablespoons walnuts, chopped
- 1 tablespoon almond, chopped
- 1 tablespoon macadamia nuts, chopped
- 3 tablespoon coconut shred
- 2 teaspoon chia seeds
- 1 tablespoon almond flour
- 2 tablespoon swerve
- 1 tablespoon coconut butter

Directions:
Preheat the oven to 360F. Meanwhile, mix up together all the ingredients in the big bowl. Stir the ingredients until you get a homogenous mixture. Line the baking tray with parchment and place the granola mixture on it. Flatten it well and put in the oven. Cook the granola for 15 minutes. Cut the cooked granola into bars.

Nutrition value/serving: calories 253, fat 22.7, fiber 6.2, carbs 11.5, protein 5

Yogurt Bowl

*Prep time: 5 minutes | **Cooking time:** 20 minutes | **Servings:** 2*

Ingredients:
- 1 cup almond yogurt
- 2 tablespoon coconut shred
- 1 tablespoon swerve
- ½ cup blackberries
- 1 oz raspberries
- 1 oz almond flakes

Directions:
Whisk the almond yogurt and freeze it for 20 minutes. Freeze the blackberries. Then combine together frozen yogurt, swerve, and blackberries in the food processor. Blend the mixture until smooth. Transfer the yogurt mixture in the serving bowls. Sprinkle the yogurt with the raspberries, coconut shred, and almond flakes.

Nutrition value/serving: calories 165, fat 11.4, fiber 4.3, carbs 12.7, protein 3.8

Morning Coffee Shake

*Prep time: 8 minutes | **Servings:** 2*

Ingredients:
- 1 cup brewed coffee
- 1 cup almond milk
- 1 tablespoon butter
- 1 teaspoon vanilla extract
- 4 ice cubes

Directions:
Put the brewed coffee, almond milk, butter, and vanilla extract in the food processor. Blend the liquid until smooth. Pour the coffee shake in the serving glasses and add ice cubes.

Nutrition value/serving: calories 334, fat 34.4, fiber 2.6, carbs 6.9, protein 3

Tofu Scramble

Prep time: 5 minutes | Cooking time: 10 minutes | Servings: 2

Ingredients:
- 10 oz firm tofu
- 1 teaspoon turmeric
- ½ white onion, diced
- 1 teaspoon garlic powder
- 1 tablespoon coconut oil
- 1 teaspoon salt
- ½ cup spinach, chopped

Directions:
Pour coconut oil in the frying pan. Add white onion and start to cook it. Then place the firm tofu over the onion and scramble it with the help of potato mash. Stir the ingredients. Add salt, turmeric, garlic powder, and spinach. Close the lid and cook the meal for 5 minutes over the medium-high heat.

Nutrition value/serving: calories 179, fat 12.9, fiber 2.4, carbs 7, protein 12.5

Zucchini Tots

Prep time: 10 minutes | Cooking time: 10 minutes | Servings: 3

Ingredients:
- 1 large zucchini, grated
- 1 tablespoon almond flour
- ½ teaspoon ground black pepper
- 1 teaspoon salt
- 1 tablespoon avocado oil

Directions:
Squeeze the grated zucchini to get rid ½ of all liquid. Put the squeezed zucchini in the bowl. Add almond flour, ground black pepper, and salt. Stir it well with the help of the fork. Pour avocado oil on the frying pan and preheat it. Make the medium size tots from the zucchini mixture. Place them in the frying pan and cook for 2 minutes from each side or until light brown.

Nutrition value/serving: calories 78, fat 5.5, fiber 2.5, carbs 6.1, protein 3.4

Fragrant Smoothie

Prep time: 10 minutes | Servings: 3

Ingredients:
- 2 tablespoons egg white protein powder
- 1 teaspoon vanilla extract
- 1 tablespoon ground cinnamon
- 1 cup coconut milk, creamed
- 1 oz almonds

Directions:
Blend the almonds until you get powder. Place the almond powder in the food processor. Add ground cinnamon, creamed coconut milk, vanilla extract, and egg white protein powder. Blend the mixture until smooth. Pour the cooked smoothie in the serving glasses. Add ice cubes if desired.

Nutrition value/serving: calories 302, fat 23.8, fiber 4.2, carbs 9.8, protein 14.6

Breakfast Bagels

Prep time: 10 minutes | Cooking time: 25 minutes | Servings: 6

Ingredients:
- 1 cup coconut flour
- ½ teaspoon baking powder
- ¾ teaspoon salt
- 5 tablespoon tahini paste
- 1 tablespoon flax meal
- 3 tablespoon water

Directions:
Stir the tahini paste in water. In the mixing bowl combine together coconut flour, baking powder, salt, and flax meal. Add tahini mixture and knead a smooth dough. Then roll up the dough with the help of the rolling pin. Line the tray with parchment. Make the bagels from the dough and transfer them on the tray. Brush the bagels with water. Preheat oven to 365F. Place the bagels in the preheated oven and cook for 25 minutes or until light brown. Chill the cooked bagels till the room temperature.

Nutrition value/serving: calories 160, fat 9.1, fiber 9.5, carbs 16.5, protein 5.1

Almond Scramble

Prep time: 7 minutes | Cooking time: 8 minutes | Servings: 2

Ingredients:
- 6 oz firm tofu
- ¼ cup almond milk
- 1 teaspoon olive oil
- 4 oz celery stalk, chopped
- 1 teaspoon salt
- 1 teaspoon chili flakes

Directions:
Preheat the frying pan well and pour olive oil inside. Add celery stalk and sprinkle it with chili flakes and salt. Fry it for 2-3 minutes over the medium heat/ Scramble tofu with the help of the fork and add in the frying pan. Stir the mixture. Add almond milk and stir it again. Close the lid and cook the meal for 5 minutes over low heat.

Nutrition value/serving: calories 158, fat 13.1, fiber 2.4, carbs 4.8, protein 8.1

Vanilla Sticks

Prep time: 10 minutes | Cooking time: 5 minutes | Servings: 4

Ingredients:
- 10 oz firm tofu
- 2 tablespoon cocoa butter
- 1 tablespoon ground cinnamon
- 1 tablespoon monk fruit
- 1 teaspoon vanilla extract
- 1 teaspoon of cocoa powder

Directions:
Cut tofu into 4 sticks. Then mix up together ground cinnamon, monk fruit, vanilla extract, and cocoa powder. Stir the mixture well. Coat the tofu sticks in the vanilla mixture well. Toss cocoa butter in the pan and preheat it. Put the vanilla tofu sticks in the preheated cocoa butter and cook for 2 minutes from each side over the high heat. Chill the tofu sticks little before serving.

Nutrition value/serving: calories 118, fat 9.8, fiber 1.7, carbs 3, protein 6

Pancakes

Prep time: 10 minutes | *Cooking time:* 10 minutes | *Servings:* 4

Ingredients:

- 1 cup almond flour
- ½ cup almond milk
- 1 tablespoon monk fruit
- 1 teaspoon vanilla extract
- 1 tablespoon pumpkin puree
- 1 tablespoon olive oil
- 1 teaspoon baking powder

Directions:

Whisk together almond flour and almond milk. Add monk fruit, vanilla extract, baking powder, and pumpkin puree. Stir the mixture until you get a smooth batter. Pour olive oil in the batter and stir little. Preheat the non-sticky pan well. Pour the ladle of the batter in the pan and make the pancake. Cook it for 1.5 minutes from each side. Repeat the same steps with all remaining batter. It is recommended to serve the pancakes hot.

Nutrition value/serving: calories 273, fat 24, fiber 3.8, carbs 8.7, protein 6.7

Green Frittata

Prep time: 10 minutes | *Cooking time:* 15 minutes | *Servings:* 3

Ingredients:

- 5 oz white mushrooms, chopped
- 1 teaspoon turmeric
- 1 teaspoon onion powder
- ½ teaspoon garlic powder
- 1 teaspoon salt
- 8 oz firm tofu
- 1 cup spinach
- 1 tomato, chopped
- 2 tablespoon olive oil
- ½ teaspoon tahini paste
- ½ cup of water

Directions:

Pour olive oil in the pan and preheat it. Place the chopped mushrooms in the preheated olive oil and start to fry them over the medium-low heat. Meanwhile, put the tofu, spinach, tahini paste, water, garlic powder, onion powder, and turmeric in the food processor. Blend the mixture until smooth. Transfer the blended green mixture over the mushrooms and stir. Add water and chopped tomatoes. Stir the meal and close the lid. Cook frittata for 5 minutes over the medium heat.

Nutrition value/serving: calories 161, fat 13.2, fiber 2, carbs 5.6, protein 8.5

Breakfast Bread

Prep time: 10 minutes | Cooking time: 30 minutes | Servings: 6

Ingredients:

- 1 cup almond flour
- ½ cup flax meal
- 1 teaspoon baking powder
- 1 teaspoon salt
- ½ cup almond milk
- 2 tablespoons coconut butter
- 1 tablespoon pumpkin seeds

Directions:

Preheat the oven to 360F. Make the bread dough: mix up together flax meal, almond flour, baking powder salt, almond milk, coconut butter, and knead the dough with the help of the cooking machine or use fingertips. When the mixture is homogenous, add pumpkin seeds and knead the dough one more time until homogenous. Place the dough in the bread pan and transfer it in the oven. Cook the breakfast bread for 30 minutes. Check the bread after 25 minutes of cooking. The cooked bread should be solid inside. Chill the breakfast bread up to 2 hours before serving. It is recommended to serve it with the mashed avocado.

Nutrition value/serving: calories 152, fat 14.1, fiber 4.5, carbs 6.6, protein 4.1

Breakfast Chocolate Balls

Prep time: 10 minutes | Cooking time: 15 minutes | Servings: 5

Ingredients:

- 1 cup almond flour
- 1 teaspoon baking powder
- 1 teaspoon lemon juice
- 2 tablespoon monk fruit
- 1 teaspoon ground nutmeg
- 1 oz dark chocolate
- 2 tablespoon butter
- 2 tablespoon heavy cream
- ¼ cup of water

Directions:

In the mixing bowl mix up together almond flour, baking powder, and lemon juice. Add monk fruit, butter, ground nutmeg, and water. Knead the soft dough. Leave the dough for 15 minutes to rest. Meanwhile, preheat the oven to 365F. Make the log from the dough and cut it into 5 pieces. Roll the balls from the dough and press them gently with the help of the hand palm. Put the dough balls on the tray and cook in the preheated oven for 12 minutes. Meanwhile, melt the chocolate on the water bath. Add heavy cream and stir well. When the balls are cooked, chill them well. You can put balls in the freezer for 10 minutes. Dip every ball in the melted chocolate mixture.

Nutrition value/serving: calories 127, fat 11.5, fiber 0.9, carbs 6.7, protein 1.8

Dill Mushroom Hats

Prep time: *10 minutes* | *Cooking time:* *15 minutes* | *Servings:* 2

Ingredients:
- 1 cup mushroom hats
- 2 teaspoon coconut butter
- 1 tablespoon fresh dill, chopped
- ½ teaspoon garlic powder
- ½ teaspoon chili flakes
- 4 oz tofu, chopped

Directions:

Peel the mushroom hats. Mix up together coconut butter, fresh dill, garlic powder, chili flakes, and chopped tofu. Stir the mixture well. Then fill the mushroom hats with tofu mixture and transfer on the tray. Cook the mushroom hats for 15 minutes at 365F.

Nutrition value/serving: calories 67, fat 3.9, fiber 1.5, carbs 4, protein 6.3

Coconut Porridge

Prep time: 5 minutes | *Cooking time: 8 hours* | *Servings: 3*

Ingredients:
- 4 tablespoon coconut shred
- 1 cup almond milk
- 4 tablespoon chia seeds
- 4 tablespoon pecans
- ½ teaspoon ground cinnamon
- 2 tablespoon monk fruit

Directions:

Pour the almond milk into3 glasses. In every glass add coconut shred, chis seeds, and ground cinnamon. Chop the pecans and add them in glasses too. Stir the porridge and leave it for 8 hours before serving.

Nutrition value/serving: calories 428, fat 42, fiber 8.5, carbs 14.1, protein 5.4

Keto Casserole

Prep time: 10 minutes | Cooking time: 15 minutes | Servings: 4

Ingredients:
- 7 oz celery stalk, chopped
- 1 teaspoon butter
- 1 teaspoon smoked paprika
- 1 teaspoon salt
- 4 oz Parmesan
- 4 eggs, beaten
- 1 tomato, sliced

Directions:
Whisk the eggs and grate Parmesan. Pour the whisked eggs in the casserole pan. Add butter, smoked paprika, salt, and chopped celery stalk. Then sprinkle the egg mixture with grated cheese and sliced tomato. Put the casserole in the preheated to 365F oven and cook for 15 minutes or until the casserole is firmed.

Nutrition value/serving: calories 175, fat 11.6, fiber 1.2, carbs 3.7, protein 15.2

Cup Muffin

Prep time: 15 minutes | Cooking time: 10 minutes | Servings: 2

Ingredients:
- ½ teaspoon baking powder
- 4 tablespoon almond flour
- 1 tablespoon coconut shred
- 1 teaspoon lemon juice
- 1 teaspoon vanilla extract
- ½ teaspoon poppy seeds
- 1 tablespoon monk fruit
- 5 tablespoons almond milk

Directions:
Mix up together all the ingredients. When you get a smooth batter, transfer it into 2 cups. Preheat oven to 365F. Place the cups in the oven and cook for 10 minutes. Then let the cooked muffins chill for 15 minutes.

Nutrition value/serving: calories 200, fat 17.6, fiber 2.8, carbs 6.8, protein 4.2

Spinach Muffin

Prep time: *15 minutes* | *Cooking time:* *12 minutes* | *Servings:* 2

Ingredients:
- ¼ cup spinach, chopped
- ¼ cup zucchini, grated
- 2 eggs, beaten
- ½ teaspoon Pink salt
- 1 teaspoon ground white pepper
- 1 teaspoon olive oil

Directions:
Whisk the eggs and combine them together with the grated zucchini and spinach. Add Pink salt and ground white pepper. Brush the muffin molds with olive oil. Transfer the spinach mixture in the muffin molds. Preheat the oven to 365F and put the muffins inside. Cook the muffins for 12 minutes or until they are firmed. Chill the spinach muffins for 10 minutes before serving.

Nutrition value/serving: calories 89, fat 6.8, fiber 0.5, carbs 1.6, protein 5.9

Lunch Recipes

Cauliflower Hash Brown Bowl
Prep time: 10 minutes | Cooking time: 10 minutes | Servings: 4

Ingredients:
- 1 cup white mushrooms, chopped
- 1 white onion, diced
- 1 tablespoon coconut oil
- 1 teaspoon Pink salt
- 1 teaspoon turmeric
- 1-pound cauliflower, shredded
- 1 teaspoon ground black pepper
- 1 teaspoon garlic powder
- ¼ cup almond milk

Directions:
Place the coconut oil in the saucepan. Add chopped mushrooms and diced onion. Sprinkle the vegetables with the turmeric, Pink salt, ground black pepper, and garlic powder. Stir and cook the ingredients for 3 minutes. After this, add shredded cauliflower and stir well. Add almond milk. Stir the mixture again. Close the lid and cook the meal for 6 minutes over the medium-high heat. When the time is over – stir the meal carefully with the help of a spatula.

Nutrition value/serving: calories 113, fat 7.3, fiber 4.3, carbs 11.2, protein 3.7

Baked Asparagus with Eggs
Prep time: 10 minutes | Cooking time: 13 minutes | Servings: 2

Ingredients:
- 2 eggs
- 8 oz asparagus
- 1 garlic clove, diced
- 1 teaspoon salt
- 1 tablespoon butter
- 1 oz almonds, chopped
- 4 tablespoon water
- ½ teaspoon dried rosemary
- 1 tablespoon chopped parsley

Directions:
Preheat the oven to 365F. Chop the asparagus roughly and sprinkle it with salt and dried rosemary. Put the chopped vegetables in the springform pan. Add butter and water. Cook the asparagus in the preheated oven for 8 minutes. Stir the vegetables every 4 minutes. Then remove the vegetables from the oven. Sprinkle them with diced garlic and almonds, stir. After this, beat the eggs over asparagus and transfer back in the oven. Cook the meal for 5 minutes more or until the eggs are firm.

Nutrition value/serving: calories 222, fat 17.4, fiber 4.4, carbs 8.6, protein 11.3

Broccoli Fritters

Prep time: *10 minutes* | *Cooking time:* *10 minutes* | *Servings:* *4*

Ingredients:
- 1-pound broccoli
- 1 teaspoon chili flakes
- 2 eggs, beaten
- 4 oz Parmesan, grated
- 2 tablespoon almond meal
- 4 tablespoon ground flax meal
- 3 tablespoon olive oil

Directions:
Chop broccoli roughly and put in the food processor. Add chili flakes, beaten eggs, grated cheese, and almond flour. Blend the mixture until you get a smooth batter. After this, make the medium balls from the batter and coat them in the flax meal. Preheat the skillet well and add olive oil. Preheat it. Cook the broccoli balls for 2minutes from each side or until light brown.

Nutrition value/serving: calories 298, fat 23.1, fiber 5.3, carbs 11.4, protein 17.2

Green Beans Salad

Prep time: *5 minutes* | *Cooking time:* *15 minutes* | *Servings:* *3*

Ingredients:
- 1 cup green beans, chopped
- 6 oz cauliflower florets
- 1 cup of water
- 1 teaspoon salt
- 1 teaspoon dried oregano
- 1 cup lettuce, chopped
- 2 tablespoon canola oil
- 1 tablespoon mustard

Directions:
In the saucepan combine together green beans and broccoli florets. Add salt, close the lid, and cook the vegetables for 10 minutes over the medium-high heat. Mean while, mix up together dried oregano, 1 tablespoon canola oil, and mustard in the mixing bowl. Whisk the mixture. Then preheat the skillet. Strain the vegetables and transfer them in the preheated skillet. Add remaining canola oil and roast for 2 minutes over the high heat. Put the chopped lettuce in the salad bowl. Add roasted vegetables and mustard mixture. Shake gently.

Nutrition value/serving: calories 130, fat 10.6, fiber 3.6, carbs 7.8, protein 2.9

Risotto

Prep time: 10 minutes | Cooking time: 25 minutes | Servings: 4

Ingredients:

- 1 teaspoon butter
- 8 oz cauliflower, riced
- 1 white onion, diced
- 1 teaspoon Pink salt
- 1 teaspoon ground black pepper
- 1 garlic clove, crushed
- 5 cremini mushrooms, chopped
- 1 tablespoon olive oil
- ½ cup almond milk
- 5 oz firmed tofu
- ½ cup of water

Directions:

Pour butter and olive oil in the saucepan and preheat. Add diced onion, ground black pepper, salt, and crushed garlic. Cook the spices for 2-3 minutes over the medium-high heat. Add chopped mushrooms, onion, and water. Close the lid and simmer the vegetables for 10 minutes. Then add riced cauliflower and almond milk. Stir gently and cook for 5 minutes more. Meanwhile, crumble tofu. Add tofu in the meal and stir well. Cook it for 5 minutes more.

Nutrition value/serving: calories 169, fat 13.2, fiber 3.4, carbs 9.9, protein 6

Eggplant Rolls

Prep time: 10 minutes | Cooking time: 5 minutes | Servings: 4

Ingredients:

- 1 large eggplant
- 1 teaspoon salt
- ½ teaspoon ground black pepper
- 1 teaspoon olive oil
- ½ teaspoon garlic powder
- 4 oz Mozzarella, sliced
- 1 green pepper

Directions:

Cut the eggplants lengthways and rub with salt and ground black pepper. Leave them for 5 minutes, Meanwhile, cut the green pepper into wedges and sprinkle with garlic powder. Preheat the grill well. Fill the eggplants with sliced Mozzarella and pepper wedges. Roll the eggplants and secure with toothpicks. Transfer them in the preheated grill and brush with the olive oil from each side. Grill the eggplant roll for 2 minutes from each side or until cooked.

Nutrition value/serving: calories 126, fat 6.4, fiber 4.7, carbs 9.5, protein 9.5

Zucchini Gratin

Prep time: *10 minutes* | *Cooking time:* *40 minutes* | *Servings: 6*

Ingredients:
- 2 zucchini, sliced
- 1 cup heavy cream
- 5 oz Cheddar cheese
- 1 teaspoon ground black pepper
- 1 teaspoon butter
- 1 tablespoon almond flour
- 1 teaspoon chili pepper
- 1 oz celery stalk, chopped

Directions:
Grate Cheddar cheese. Grease the pan with butter. Place the layer of sliced zucchini in the greased pan. Then sprinkle it over with Cheddar cheese and celery stalk. Season with ground black pepper and chili pepper. Repeat the steps until you use all the ingredients. After this, mix up together heavy cream and almond flour. Pour the liquid over the vegetables. Preheat the oven to 365F. Cook gratin for 40 minutes.

Nutrition value/serving: calories 209, fat 18.3, fiber 1.4, carbs 4.5, protein 8.2

Zucchini Boats

Prep time: *10 minutes* | *Cooking time:* *15 minutes* | *Servings: 2*

Ingredients:
- 1 large zucchini
- 6 oz goat cheese
- 1 teaspoon chopped dill
- ½ teaspoon white pepper
- 1 tablespoon tomato paste

Directions:
Cut the zucchini into halves and remove the flesh from it. Then crumble the goat cheese and mix it up with chopped dill, white pepper, and tomato paste. Stir the mixture. Fill the zucchini halves with the cheese mixture. Wrap the zucchini in the foil. Preheat oven to 375F and put the zucchini inside. Cook the meal for 15 minutes or until the zucchini is tender.

Nutrition value/serving: calories 419, fat 30.6, fiber 2.3, carbs 9.4, protein 28.4

Eggplant Gratin

*Prep time: 10 minutes | **Cooking time:** 30 minutes | Servings: 4*

Ingredients:

- 1 large eggplant
- 4 oz Parmesan, grated
- 6 oz Cheddar cheese, shredded
- 1 white onion, diced
- ½ cup heavy cream
- 1 teaspoon minced garlic
- 1 teaspoon ground black pepper
- 1 teaspoon butter
- 1 tablespoon chives

Directions:

Chop eggplant and sprinkle it with ground black pepper and minced garlic. Grease the pan with butter and place the chopped eggplants inside. Then make the layer of Cheddar cheeseover the eggplant. Sprinkle the cheese with chives and diced onion. Sprinkle the onion with grated Parmesan. Pour the heavy cream over the cheese. Cover the gratin with foil and secure the lids. Preheat the oven to 365F and put the gratin inside. Cook the meal for 30 minutes.

Nutrition value/serving: calories 365, fat 26.9, fiber 4.8, carbs 11.9, protein 21.6

Greek Salad

Prep time: 7 minutes | Servings: 3

Ingredients:

- 2 tomatoes, chopped
- 1 cucumber, chopped
- 4 oz Feta cheese, chopped
- 1 tablespoon olive oil
- 1 tablespoon chopped dill
- ½ teaspoon dried oregano
- ½ teaspoon ground black pepper

Directions:

In the mixing bowl combine together chopped Feta, cucumber, and tomatoes. Take the separate bowl and whisk together olive oil, dried oregano and ground black pepper. Add the olive oil mixture in the vegetable bowl. Then add chopped dill and mix up the salad well.

Nutrition value/serving: calories 174, fat 13.1, fiber 1.8, carbs 9.3, protein 7

Portobello Mushrooms

Prep time: 8 minutes | Cooking time: 8 minutes | Servings: 1

Ingredients:
- 1 portobello mushroom hat
- 2 quail eggs
- 3 oz Tofu, crumbled
- 1 teaspoon coconut oil
- ½ teaspoon ground black pepper
- ¼ white onion, diced

Directions:

Preheat oven to 365F. Put coconut oil in the mushroom hat. Sprinkle it with ground black pepper and crumbled Tofu. Then add diced onion and beat the eggs. Place the mushroom hat in the tray and transfer in the oven. Cook the meal for 8 minutes.

Nutrition value/serving: calories 161, fat 10.1, fiber 2.6, carbs 7.8, protein 12.7

Avocado Eggs

Prep time: 5 minutes | Cooking time: 12 minutes | Servings: 2

Ingredients:
- 1 avocado, halved
- 2 eggs
- ½ teaspoon salt
- ¼ teaspoon ground black pepper
- 2 teaspoon almond butter

Directions:

Sprinkle the avocado halves with salt, ground black pepper, and add almond butter. Beat the eggs in the avocado holes. Place the avocado halves in the tray and transfer in the preheated to the 360F oven. Cook the meal for 12 minutes. The meal is cooked when the avocado is semi-cooked and eggs are firm.

Nutrition value/serving: calories 367, fat 33, fiber 8.4, carbs 12.2, protein 10.9

Kale Soup

Prep time: 10 minutes | Cooking time: 25 minutes | Servings: 5

Ingredients:

- 2 cups almond milk
- 1 cup kale
- 6 oz cauliflower florets
- 2 oz green pepper, chopped
- 1/3 white onion, diced
- 1 oz celery stalk, chopped
- 1 tablespoon coconut butter
- 1 teaspoonpecan, chopped
- 1cup of water
- 1 teaspoon curry paste
- 1 teaspoon tahini paste
- 1 teaspoon ground black pepper
- 1 teaspoon salt
- ½ teaspoon chili pepper
- ½ teaspoon dried oregano

Directions:

Preheat the oven to 365F. Place the cauliflower florets in the tray and sprinkle with curry paste. Mix up the vegetables carefully and transfer in the oven. Cook the cauliflower for 15 minutes. Meanwhile, toss coconut butter in the saucepan. Add celery stalk, white onion, green pepper, and tahini paste. Stir the ingredients and cook over the medium-low heat for 5 minutes. Then add dried oregano, chili pepper, salt, ground black pepper, and chopped pecans. Chop the kale and add in the saucepan too. Add water and stir well. Cook it for 10 minutes. When the cauliflower is cooked – transfer it in the blender and blend well. Put the blended cauliflower in the kale saucepan and add almond milk. When the soup starts to boil, use the hand blender to make it smooth. Boil it for 2-3 minutes more.

Nutrition value/serving: calories 281, fat 26.6, fiber 4.5, carbs 11.7, protein 4.1

Spinach Pie

Prep time: 10 minutes | Cooking time: 25 minutes | Servings: 6

Ingredients:

- 3 cups spinach, chopped
- 8 oz Parmesan, grated
- 1 teaspoon ground white pepper
- 1 teaspoon garlic powder
- 4 eggs, whisked

Directions:

Mix up together grated Parmesan and chopped spinach. Add ground white pepper and garlic powder. Stir the mixture. Preheat oven to 360F. Place the spinach mixture in the glass pan and flatten gently. Pour the whisked egg over the spinach mixture. Transfer the spinach pie in the oven and cook for 25 minutes. Chill the cooked pie till the room temperature.

Nutrition value/serving: calories 169, fat 11.1, fiber 0.5, carbs 2.7, protein 16.4

Tofu Wraps

Prep time: 10 minutes | Cooking time: 15 minutes | Servings: 4

Ingredients:

- 8 oz firmed tofu
- ½ cup white mushrooms, chopped
- 1 tablespoon chives, chopped
- 1 teaspoon salt
- 1 teaspoon paprika
- 1 tablespoon coconut butter
- ¼ cup almond milk
- 1 teaspoon curry paste
- 1 cup lettuce leaves

Directions:

Preheat coconut butter in the saucepan. Meanwhile, chop tofu into tiny pieces. Add the chopped tofu and white mushrooms in the saucepan. Sprinkle the ingredients with chives, salt, paprika, andcurry paste. Stir well and cook for 5 minutes. After this, add almond milk and close the lid. Cook the tofu mixture for 10 minutes over the low-medium heat. Then chill the mixture till the room temperature. Fill the lettuce leaves with the tofu mixture.

Nutrition value/serving: calories 116, fat 9.3, fiber 1.7, carbs 4.2, protein 5.7

Bok Choy Salad

Prep time: 10 minutes | Cooking time: 10 minutes | Servings: 4

Ingredients:

- 1 tablespoon lemon juice
- 2 tablespoon sesame oil
- 1 teaspoon salt
- ½ teaspoon chili flakes
- 1 tablespoon apple cider vinegar
- 1 cup bok choy
- 10 oz firmed tofu
- 1 tablespoon almond butter
- 1 teaspoon sesame seeds

Directions:

Cut tofu into cubes and sprinkle with lemon juice, sesame oil, salt, and chili flakes. Mix up the tofu cubes well and leave for 5 minutes to marinate. Preheat the skillet well. Toss tofu cubes in the skillet and roast them on the high heat for 30 seconds from each side. Transfer cooked tofu cubes in the salad bowl. Chop the bok choy roughly and transfer in the skillet. Add almond butter and roast it for 5 minutes. Stir it from time to time. Transfer bok choy in the salad bowl. Add apple cider vinegar and stir well. It is recommended to serve the salad warm.

Nutrition value/serving: calories 143, fat 12.5, fiber 1.3, carbs 2.6, protein 7.1

Avocado Pie

Prep time: 15 minutes | Cooking time: 30 minutes | Servings: 6

Ingredients:
- 1 cup almond flour
- ½ teaspoon baking powder
- 1 teaspoon lemon juice
- 1 teaspoon ground black pepper
- 1 tablespoon olive oil
- ¼ cup almond milk
- 1 avocado, chopped
- 2 medium celery stalks
- ½ white onion, diced
- 4 eggs, whisked

Directions:
In the food processor mix up together almond flour, baking powder, lemon juice, ground black pepper, olive oil, and almond milk. Blend it until you get a soft dough ball. Leave the dough ball for 10 minutes to rest. Meanwhile, make the filling: chop the celery stalk and combine it together with avocado and diced onion. Cut the dough into 2 parts. Roll up every dough part with the help of the rolling pin. Place the first dough part in the round pan. Place the filling over the dough. Roll up the second dough part and cover the filling. Secure the pie edges with the help of the fork. Brush the pie with water and transfer in the preheated to a 365F oven. Cook the pie for 30 minutes or until golden brown. Chill the pie till the room temperature.

Nutrition value/serving: calories 187, fat 16.5, fiber 3.5, carbs 6.4, protein 5.8

Turnip Gratin

Prep time: 10 minutes | Cooking time: 25 minutes | Servings: 6

Ingredients:
- 1 tablespoon dill, chopped
- 10 oz turnip, peeled, chopped
- 1 garlic clove, diced
- 1 white onion, diced
- 1 cup heavy cream
- 8 oz Cheddar cheese
- 1 teaspoon white pepper
- 1 teaspoon olive oil

Directions:
Brush the gratin pan with olive oil. Then mix up together shredded cheese and chopped dill. Put the layer of chopped turnip in the gratin pan and sprinkle it over with the diced onion and garlic. Add white pepper and cheese. Pour the heavy cream over the gratin. Preheat the oven to 365F. Cook the gratin for 25 minutes. When the gratin is cooked, use the kitchen torch to make the crunchy crust.

Nutrition value/serving: calories 251, fat 20.8, fiber 1.4, carbs 6.5, protein 10.6

Gnocchi

Prep time: *10 minutes* | *Cooking time:* *5 minutes* | *Servings:* 2

Ingredients:
- 7 oz Mozzarella
- 2 egg yolks
- 1 teaspoon dried parsley
- 1 tablespoon olive oil

Directions:
Grate Mozzarella cheese and put in the bowl. Melt the cheese in the microwave oven. Then stir it constantly and add egg yolks gradually. When the mixture is homogenous, add dried parsley. Stir it. Make the long logs from the cheese mixture and cut them into 1-inch pieces. Press every cheese piece with a fork gently. Preheat the olive oil in the skillet. Put the cheese pieces in the hot oil and cook for 30 seconds from each side or until light brown.

Nutrition value/serving: calories 394, fat 29, fiber 0, carbs 4.2, protein 30.7

Spinach Soup

Prep time: *10 minutes* | *Cooking time:* *10 minutes* | *Servings:* 2

Ingredients:
- 1 ½ cup full-fat milk
- 1 white onion, diced
- 1 teaspoon chili flakes
- 1 tablespoon mustard
- 1 tablespoon olive oil
- 1 teaspoon salt
- 1 cup spinach, chopped
- ½ teaspoon ground red pepper

Directions:
Preheat saucepan well. Pour olive oil inside and add diced onion. Start to cook onion over the medium-high heat. Add chili flakes, salt, and ground red pepper. Cook the onion for 3 minutes. Then add chopped spinach and ½ cup of milk. Close the lid and cook it for 5 minutes. After this, add all remaining full-fat milk and blend the mixture to get a creamy texture. Boil soup for 2 minutes more. Ladle soup into the bowls and add mustard.

Nutrition value/serving: calories 135, fat 9.8, fiber 1.9, carbs 10.3, protein 2.9

Eggplant Pizza

Prep time: *10 minutes* | *Cooking time:* *12 minutes* | *Servings:* *2*

Ingredients:

- 1 large eggplant
- 1 tomato, sliced
- 4 oz Cheddar, shredded
- 2 teaspoon olive oil
- ½ teaspoon salt
- 2 tablespoons olives
- ¼ teaspoon dried basil

Directions:

Slice the eggplant into thick slices. Rub every slice with salt and olive oil. Leave the vegetables for 5 minutes. Preheat the oven to 365F. Line the tray with baking paper. Place the eggplant slices on the tray. Then put tomato slices over eggplants. Sprinkle them with dried basil. Slice the olives and put them over tomatoes. Add shredded cheese. Cook the eggplant pizzas for 12 minutes or until light brown.

Nutrition value/serving: calories 211, fat 10, fiber 8.7, carbs 16.3, protein 16.4

Falafel

Prep time: *10 minutes* | *Cooking time:* *10 minutes* | *Servings:* *2*

Ingredients:

- 1 egg, beaten
- 8 oz cauliflower puree
- 1 teaspoon almonds, grinded
- ¼ teaspoon ground cumin
- ¼ teaspoon ground coriander
- 1 teaspoon tahini paste
- 1 teaspoon olive oil
- 1 tablespoon dried dill
- 1 tablespoon almond flour
- ½ teaspoon minced garlic
- 1 tablespoon lemon juice

Directions:

Combine together cauliflower puree and beaten egg. Add grinded almonds, ground cumin, ground coriander, and dried dill. After this, add minced garlic and mix up the mixture until homogenous. Make the medium balls from the cauliflower mixture and coat them in the almond flour. Press the falafel gently. Preheat the skillet well. Add olive oil. Put falafel in the skillet and cook for 3 minutes from each side or until golden brown. Mix up together lemon juice and tahini paste. Transfer the cooked falafel on the plate and sprinkle with the tahini-lemon sauce.

Nutrition value/serving: calories 188, fat 13.7, fiber 5, carbs 11.3, protein 9.1

Egg Salad

Prep time: 10 *minutes* | *Servings: 2*

Ingredients:

- 4 eggs, boiled
- 1 avocado, peeled, chopped
- 1 tablespoon mustard
- 5 tablespoon almond milk
- 1 tablespoon apple cider vinegar
- ½ teaspoon smoked paprika
- 1 cup lettuce, chopped

Directions:

Make the sauce for salad: mix up together almond milk, apple cider vinegar, mustard, and smoked paprika. Then peel the eggs and chop them. Put the eggs in the salad bowl. Add chopped avocado and lettuce. Pour the sauce over the salad and stir with the help of two spoons.

Nutrition value/serving: calories 450, fat 39, fiber 8.8, carbs 14.6, protein 15.5

Quesadillas

Prep time: 10 *minutes* | *Cooking time:* 20 *minutes* | *Servings: 4*

Ingredients:

- ¼ cup Psyllium husk powder
- 1 tablespoon almond flour
- ¾ teaspoon salt
- 3 eggs, beaten
- ¼ cup spinach, chopped
- 5 oz Cheddar cheese, shredded
- 1 tablespoon olive oil

Directions:

Make tortilla: mix up together almond flour, Psyllium husk powder, salt, and eggs, Knead dough. Preheat oven to 375F. Roll out the dough and make 8 tortillas Line the tray with baking paper and place tortillas on it. Transfer the tray in the oven and cook for 7 minutes. Meanwhile, mix up together shredded cheese and spinach. Preheat the skillet well and add olive oil. Transfer 1 tortillas in the skillet. Add a small amount of spinach mixture and cover with the second tortilla. Cook quesadillas for 1 minute from each side (the cheese inside the tortillas should be melted). Repeat the steps with all tortillas.

Nutrition value/serving: calories 290, fat 22, fiber 7.8, carbs 10.3, protein 14.5

Cheese Rolls

Prep time: 10 minutes | Servings: 4

Ingredients:
- 10 oz Provolone cheese
- 2 tablespoon butter, softened
- ½ teaspoon minced garlic
- 2 tablespoon fresh dill, chopped
- ¼ teaspoon ground paprika

Directions:

Slice cheese into large squares. Then churn together butter, minced garlic, chopped dill, and ground paprika. Spread the cheese slices with churned butter mixture. Roll the cheese slices.

Nutrition value/serving: calories 304, fat 24.7, fiber 0.3, carbs 2.6, protein 18.5

Side Dishes

Mashed Cauliflower

Prep time: 10 minutes | *Cooking time:* 15 minutes | *Servings:* 4

Ingredients:

- 2 teaspoon minced garlic
- 10 oz cauliflower
- 1 teaspoon lemon juice
- 3 tablespoon almond milk
- 1 teaspoon salt
- ½ teaspoon chili flakes
- 2 cups of water

Directions:

Pour water in the saucepan and add cauliflower. Close the lid and boil it for 15 minutes or until the vegetable is soft. Then strain the cauliflower and transfer it in the blender. Add minced garlic, almond milk, lemon juice, salt, and chili flakes. Blend the vegetable until smooth and soft. Transfer the cooked mashed cauliflower in the serving bowls.

Nutrition value/serving: calories 46, fat 2.8, fiber 2.1, carbs 4.9, protein 1.8

Fragrant Cauliflower Steaks

Prep time: 10 minutes | *Cooking time:* 10 minutes | *Servings:* 6

Ingredients:

- 2-pound cauliflower head
- 1 teaspoon Taco seasoning
- 1 teaspoon ground thyme
- 1 tablespoon butter
- 4 oz Parmesan, grated

Directions:

Preheat the grill to 365F. Meanwhile, slice the cauliflower head into steaks. Rub every cauliflower steak with Taco seasoning and ground thyme. Place the steaks on the grill and grill for 2 minutes from each side. After this, rub the cauliflower with butter and cook for 1 minute more from each side. Then sprinkle the cauliflower steaks with grated cheese and cook for 3 minutes only on one side.

Nutrition value/serving: calories 118, fat 6.1, fiber 3.8, carbs 9.1, protein 9.1

Fried Cheese

Prep time: *10 minutes* | *Cooking time: 5 minutes* | *Servings: 6*

Ingredients:

- 1-pound goat cheese log
- 1/3 cup almond flour
- 1 egg, whisked
- 1 teaspoon chili pepper
- ½ teaspoon garlic powder
- 1 tablespoon olive oil

Directions:

Cut the goat cheese into medium pieces. Then mix up together almond flour, chili pepper, and garlic powder. Stir it. Dip the goat cheese pieces in the whisked egg. Then coat them in the almond flour mixture. Preheat the skillet and pour olive oil inside. When the olive oil is hot, place the goat cheese inside and cook for 30 seconds from each side. Serve the cooked side dish hot.

Nutrition value/serving: calories 362, fat 28.4, fiber 0.2, carbs 2.3, protein 24.4

Cabbage Salad

Prep time: *8 minutes* | *Cooking time: 5 minutes* | *Servings: 2*

Ingredients:

- 8 oz white cabbage, shredded
- ½ avocado, peeled
- 2 tablespoons lemon juice
- 1 teaspoon avocado oil
- ¼ cup spinach, chopped
- 3 tablespoon water

Directions:

Place avocado, lemon juice, spinach, avocado oil, and water in the blender. Blend the mixture until smooth. Place the cabbage in the salad bowl. Pour the green mixture over the cabbage. Mix up the salad well and let it marinate for at least 5 minutes.

Nutrition value/serving: calories 156, fat 12.4, fiber 6.4, carbs 11.4, protein 2.6

Hummus

Prep time: 10 *minutes* | *Cooking time:* 15 *minutes* | *Servings:* 6

Ingredients:

- 2-pound cauliflower head
- 1 teaspoon salt
- 1 teaspoon garlic powder
- 1 teaspoon chili flakes
- 3 tablespoon olive oil
- 1 tablespoon tahini paste
- 1 cup of water

Directions:

Boil cauliflower head in 1 cup of water for 15 minutes or until tender. Meanwhile, mix up together salt, garlic powder, chili flakes, olive oil, and tahini paste. Strain the cauliflower. Leave 5 tablespoons of cauliflower water. Blend the vegetable until you get a mashed mixture. Add 5 tablespoons of remaining cauliflower water and tahinipaste mixture. Blend the hummus for 2 minutes more. Transfer it in the bowl.

Nutrition value/serving: calories 114, fat 8.5, fiber 4.1, carbs 8.9, protein 3.5

Roasted Halloumi

Prep time: 8 *minutes* | *Cooking time:* 5 *minutes* | *Servings:* 3

Ingredients:

- 10 oz halloumi cheese
- 1 tablespoon olive oil
- 1 teaspoon ground black pepper
- ½ teaspoon dried oregano
- ¼ teaspoon dried cilantro

Directions:

Preheat grill to 375F. Meanwhile, mix up together olive oil, ground black pepper, dried oregano, and dried cilantro. Brush the cheese with the olive oil mixture from each side. Place Halloumi cheese on the grill and cook it for 2.5 minutes from each side.

Nutrition value/serving: calories 387, fat 32.9, fiber 0.3, carbs 3, protein 20.5

Roasted Cabbage

Prep time: 10 minutes | Cooking time: 15 minutes | Servings: 3

Ingredients:
- 11 oz white cabbage
- 1 tablespoon olive oil
- 1 teaspoon white pepper
- 1 teaspoon onion powder

Directions:
Cut the white cabbage into wedges. Rub the vegetable with white pepper and onion powder. Then sprinkle with olive oil. Preheat the oven to 375F. Place the cabbage wedges in the tray and transfer in the preheated oven. Cook the side dish for 15 minutes or until the edges of the cabbage are light brown.

Nutrition value/serving: calories 71, fat 4.8, fiber 2.8, carbs 7.1, protein 1.5

Deviled Eggs

Prep time: 10 minutes | Cooking time: 6 minutes | Servings: 3

Ingredients:
- 3 eggs
- 1 tablespoon mustard
- 1 teaspoon chives, chopped
- ¾ teaspoon turmeric

Directions:
Boil the eggs for 6 minutes. Meanwhile, mix p together chives, turmeric, and mustard. When the eggs are cooked, chill them in icy water and peel. Cut the eggs into halves. Remove the egg yolks and add them in the mustard mixture. Mash it until smooth. Fill the egg whites with the egg yolk mixture.

Nutrition value/serving: calories 82, fat 5.5, fiber 0.7, carbs 2, protein 6.5

Fried Broccoli

*Prep time: 7 minutes | **Cooking time**: 13 minutes | **Servings**: 4*

Ingredients:

- 2 cups broccoli florets
- 1 teaspoon onion powder
- 2 tablespoon coconut oil
- 1 teaspoon almond flakes
- 1 teaspoon salt

Directions:

Preheat the oven to 365F. Place the broccoli florets in the tray. Add coconut oil, almond flakes, salt, and onion powder. Mix up the broccoli well. Transfer the tray in the oven and cook for 10 minutes. Then stir the broccoli and cook it for 2-3 minutes more.

Nutrition value/serving: calories 86, fat 7.8, fiber 1.4, carbs 3.7, protein 1.7

Brussel Sprouts with Nuts

*Prep time: 10 minutes | **Cooking time**: 30 minutes | **Servings**: 4*

Ingredients:

- 2 cups Brussel sprouts
- 3 oz pecans, chopped
- 3 tablespoon coconut oil
- 1 teaspoon salt
- 1 teaspoon garlic powder
- 1 teaspoon cayenne pepper

Directions:

Cut Brussel sprouts into halves and place in the tray. Mix up together coconut oil, salt, garlic powder, and cayenne pepper. Put the mixture over Brussel sprouts. Add pecans. Preheat the oven to 360F. Put the tray with Brussel sprouts in the oven and cook for 30 minutes or until sprouts are tender.

Nutrition value/serving: calories 259, fat 25.6, fiber 4.1, carbs 7.8, protein 4

Zucchini Pasta

Prep time: 10 *minutes* | *Cooking time:* 5 *minutes* | *Servings:* 4

Ingredients:
- 2 zucchini, trimmed
- 1 tablespoon olive oil
- ¼ cup almond milk
- ½ teaspoon salt
- ½ teaspoon ground black pepper
- ¼ cup spinach
- ½ avocado, peeled

Directions:
Make the noodles from zucchini with the help of spiralizer. Preheat the olive oil in the skillet and add zucchini noodles. Sprinkle "noodles" with almond milk, salt, and ground black pepper. Cook the mixture for 3 minutes over the medium-high heat. Meanwhile, blend together spinach and avocado. Add the avocado mixture in the zucchini noodles and stir until homogenous. Cook the meal for 2 minutes more.

Nutrition value/serving: calories 133, fat 12.2, fiber 3.2, carbs 6.5, protein 2.1

Shirataki Noodles

Prep time: 10 *minutes* | *Cooking time:* 5 *minutes* | *Servings:* 3

Ingredients:
- 10 oz shirataki noodles
- 1 cup of coconut milk
- 1 tablespoon lemon juice
- ¾ teaspoon ground ginger
- ¼ teaspoon cayenne pepper
- ½ teaspoon salt

Directions:
In the saucepan combine together coconut milk. Lemon juice, ground ginger, cayenne pepper, and salt. Stir it, close the lid and cook over the high heat until it starts to boil. After this, add shirataki noodles, stir gently, and close the lid. Cook the noodles for 15 minutes. Strain the cooked noodles.

Nutrition value/serving: calories 207, fat 19.2, fiber 11.9, carbs 4.9, protein 2.6

Low Carb Baked Vegetables

Prep time: 10 minutes | *Cooking time:* 25 minutes | *Servings:* 4

Ingredients:

- 2 green peppers
- 1 cup white mushrooms
- 1 white onion, peeled
- 1 eggplant
- 1 teaspoon cayenne pepper
- 1 tablespoon almond butter
- ½ teaspoon salt

Directions:

Chop the green peppers and mushrooms roughly. Then peel the eggplant and chop it too. Combine together all the ingredients in the mixing bowl. Add salt and cayenne pepper. Stir well. Then cut the onion into 4 parts and separate into the petals. Add it into the vegetable mix. Preheat the oven to 365F. Line the baking tray with baking paper. Put all the vegetables on the tray and flatten them. Add almond butter and put in the oven. Bake thevegetables for 25 minutes or until they are tender.

Nutrition value/serving: calories 81, fat 2.7, fiber 6.3, carbs 13.6, protein 3.4

Rutabaga Swirls

Prep time: 5 minutes | *Cooking time:* 5 minutes | *Servings:* 4

Ingredients:

- 8 oz rutabaga, peeled
- 1 tablespoon almond butter
- ½ teaspoon cayenne pepper
- ¾ teaspoon salt

Directions:

Cut rutabaga into very thin strips. Sprinkle the strips with cayenne pepper and salt. Stir well. Preheat the skillet and add almond butter. Melt it. Add rutabaga strips and roast them for 5 minutes over the medium-high heat. Stir the strips constantly. When the rutabaga swirls are light brown – they are cooked.

Nutrition value/serving: calories 46, fat 2.4, fiber 1.9, carbs 5.5, protein 1.6

Fettuccine

Prep time: 10 minutes | Cooking time: 4 minutes | Servings: 1

Ingredients:
- 1 zucchini
- ¾ teaspoon salt
- ¾ teaspoon ground paprika
- 2 tablespoon almond milk

Directions:
Wash and trim zucchini. Then cut it into halves and remove the seeds. With the help of potato peeler slice the zucchini on fettuccine noodles. Transfer the noodles in the pan, add salt, ground paprika, and almond milk. Simmer fettuccine over the medium heat for 4 minutes. Then sprinkle the cooked meal with ground paprika and stir gently.

Nutrition value/serving: calories 105, fat 7.7, fiber 3.4, carbs 9.1, protein 3.3

French Fries

Prep time: 8 minutes | Cooking time: 15 minutes | Servings: 5

Ingredients:
- 3 cups Jicama fries
- 1 teaspoon onion powder
- 1 teaspoon garlic powder
- 1 teaspoon turmeric
- 1 teaspoon smoked paprika
- ½ teaspoon salt
- 3 tablespoons avocado oil

Directions:
Place Jicama fries into the mixing bowl. Add onion powder, garlic powder, turmeric, and smoked paprika. Then add salt and shake the mixture until homogenous. Preheat the oven to 365F. Make the layer of Jicama fries in the tray and sprinkle avocado oil. Use 2 trays if needed. Place the tray in the oven and bake fries for 15 minutes or until light brown.

Nutrition value/serving: calories 45, fat 1.2, fiber 4.2, carbs 8.1, protein 0.9

Broccoli Fritters

Prep time: 10 minutes | Cooking time: 5 minutes | Servings: 4

Ingredients:

- 2 tablespoon flax meal
- ½ teaspoon salt
- 1 cup broccoli
- 1 egg, beaten
- 1 teaspoon ground black pepper
- ½ cup almond flour
- 1 tablespoon olive oil
- 3 oz tofu, crumbled

Directions:

Blend broccoli until smooth. Then add salt, flax meal, beaten egg, ground black pepper, and tofu. Blend the mixture till you get the homogenous texture. Make the medium fritters from the broccoli mixture. Coat every fritter in almond flour. Preheat olive oil in the skillet. Roast broccoli fritters for 2 minutes from each side or till light brown.

Nutrition value/serving: calories 105, fat 8.6, fiber 2.3, carbs 4, protein 5.3

Spinach in Cream

Prep time: 8 minutes | Cooking time: 15 minutes | Servings: 4

Ingredients:

- 3 cups spinach
- 1 cup heavy cream
- 1 teaspoon salt
- ½ teaspoon minced garlic
- 4 oz Provolone cheese

Directions:

Chop spinach and put in a saucepan. Add salt and minced garlic. Pour heavy cream in spinach, stir gently, close the lid and simmer for 10 minutes. Stir it from time to time. Meanwhile, shred cheese. Add shredded cheese in the saucepan and stir until homogenous. Remove the saucepan from the heat and leave it to rest for 5 minutes.

Nutrition value/serving: calories 209, fat 18.7, fiber 0.5, carbs 2.4, protein 8.5

Dill Radish

*Prep time: 10 minutes | **Cooking time:** 15 minutes | **Servings:** 4*

Ingredients:

- 2 cups radish
- 1 tablespoon coconut oil
- 1 teaspoon salt
- ¼ cup of coconut milk
- 2 tablespoon dried dill

Directions:

Wash and trim radish. Then cut them into halves and sprinkle with salt, coconut milk, coconut oil, and dried dill. Mix up the radish carefully. Place the radish in the tray in one layer. Preheat the oven to 350F and put the tray inside. Cook radish for 15 minutes or until the edges of the radish starts to be light brown.

Nutrition value/serving: calories 77, fat 7.1, fiber 1.5, carbs 3.7, protein 1

Curry Rice

*Prep time: 5 minutes | **Cooking time:** 15 minutes | **Servings:** 2*

Ingredients:

- 1 tablespoon curry paste
- ½ pound cauliflower, riced
- 1 teaspoon salt
- 1 tablespoon almond butter
- 1 cup of water

Directions:

Pour water in the saucepan. Add all the remaining ingredients and close the lid. Cook rice for 15 minutes. Then strain the rice and transfer in the serving bowls.

Nutrition value/serving: calories 128, fat 9, fiber 3.6, carbs 9.6, protein 4.3

Garlic Artichokes

Prep time: 5 minutes | Cooking time: 15 minutes | Servings: 2

Ingredients:

- 1 teaspoon minced garlic
- 2 artichokes, trimmed
- ½ teaspoon salt
- 1 tablespoon canola oil

Directions:

Rub the artichokes with minced garlic, salt, and canola oil. Place the vegetables in the pan. Transfer the pan in preheated to the 350F oven. Cook the side dish for 15 minutes. Cooked artichokes should be tender but not soft.

Nutrition value/serving: calories 124, fat 7.2, fiber 6.9, carbs 14, protein 4.3

Turnip Slaw

Prep time: 15 minutes | Cooking time: 5 minutes | Servings: 4

Ingredients:

- 11 oz turnip, peeled
- ½ carrot, peeled
- 1 tablespoon lemon juice
- 1 tablespoon fresh dill, chopped
- 1 tablespoon keto mayonnaise
- ¼ teaspoon ground black pepper

Directions:

Grate turnip into rough pieces or cut into thin strips. Then grate the carrot. Mix up together all the vegetables. Add lemon juice, chopped dill, mayonnaise, and ground black pepper. Stir the salad and leave for 10 minutes to marinate.

Nutrition value/serving: calories 28, fat 0.1, fiber 1.8, carbs 6.4, protein 1

Sauteed Cabbage

Prep time: 10 minutes | *Cooking time:* 35 minutes | *Servings:* 5

Ingredients:

- 1-pound cabbage, shredded
- 1 teaspoon salt
- 1 teaspoon smoked paprika
- ½ onion, diced
- 1 teaspoon tomato paste
- 1 cup almond milk
- 1 tablespoon macadamia nuts, crushed

Directions:

Pour almond milk in the saucepan and bring it to boil. Add salt, smoked paprika, shredded cabbage, tomato paste, and diced onion. Stir until the cabbage gets the light red color. Close the lid and cook cabbage for 10 minutes over the medium heat. Then add macadamia nuts, stir, and cook for 25 minutes more over the low heat.

Nutrition value/serving: calories 152, fat 12.9, fiber 3.9, carbs 9.6, protein 2.6

Spiced Rutabaga

Prep time: 10 minutes | Cooking time: 10 minutes | Servings: 3

Ingredients:
- 1 teaspoon cayenne pepper
- ½ teaspoon salt
- 1 teaspoon dried rosemary
- 1 teaspoon dried oregano
- 1 teaspoon dried dill
- 12 oz rutabaga, peeled
- 2 tablespoons sesame oil

Directions:

Cut rutabaga into halves. Sprinklehalves with dried rosemary, salt, cayenne pepper, dill, and oregano. Put theedges on the preheated to 360F grill and sprinkle with sesame oil. Grill rutabaga for 10 minutes. Flip rutabaga halves from time to time.

Nutrition value/serving: calories 128, fat 9.4, fiber 3.6, carbs 10.7, protein 1.5

Swiss Chard

Prep time: 8 minutes | Cooking time: 15 minutes | Servings: 2

Ingredients:
- 2 cups swiss chard
- 1 tablespoon olive oil
- 1 teaspoon salt
- ½ teaspoon ground black pepper

Directions:

Chop swiss chard and transfer in the saucepan. Add salt, olive oil, and ground black pepper. Stir gently, close the lid, and saute vegetables for 15 minutes over the medium heat. Stir the vegetable time to time while cooking.

Nutrition value/serving: calories 68, fat 7.1, fiber 0.7, carbs 1.7, protein 0.7

Main Dishes

Enchiladas

*Prep time: 10 minutes | **Cooking time:** 20 minutes | **Servings:** 4*

Ingredients:
- ½ cup almond flour
- ¼ cup of coconut milk
- ½ teaspoon baking powder
- 1 teaspoon olive oil
- 1 avocado, chopped
- 8oz Cheddar, shredded
- 1 green pepper, chopped
- ½ cup heavy cream

Directions:

Mix up together almond flour, coconut milk, baking powder, and olive oil. Whisk the mixture to get batter. Preheat non-stick skillet. Ladle one ladle of the batter in the skillet and make a crepe. Flip it after 1 minute of cooking onto another side. Cook the crepe for 30 seconds more or until cooked. Make the same steps with remaining batter. After this, mix up together shredded cheese, chopped pepper, avocado, and heavy cream. Stir it. Put the cheese mixture over every crepe and roll. Place the rolled crepes in the pan and cover with the foil. Secure edges. Transfer the pan in the preheated to 350F oven and cook for 15 minutes. When the cheese is melted – the meal is cooked.

Nutrition value/serving: calories 343, fat 27.6, fiber 5, carbs 9.8, protein 17.2

Keto Satay

*Prep time: 15 minutes | **Cooking time:** 5 minutes | **Servings:** 4*

Ingredients:
- 14 oz tofu
- 2 tablespoon olive oil
- ½ teaspoon minced garlic
- 1 teaspoon ground black pepper
- 1 tablespoon tahini paste
- 1 tablespoon water
- 1 teaspoon apple cider vinegar
- 1 teaspoon sesame seeds

Directions:

Cut tofu into cubes. Sprinkle tofu with minced garlic, olive oil, ground black pepper, and apple cider vinegar. Leave tofu for 10 minutes to marinate. Meanwhile, preheat grill to 360F. Put tofu in the grill and cook for 2 minutes from each side. Make the sauce: mix up together tahini paste, water, and sesame seeds. Place the cooked tofu on the plate and sprinkle with tahini sauce.

Nutrition value/serving: calories 158, fat 13.6, fiber 1.5, carbs 3.1, protein 9

Zucchini Tart

Prep time: 15 minutes | *Cooking time:* 25 minutes | *Servings:* 8

Ingredients:

- 1 zucchini
- 1 cup ricotta cheese
- 1 cup coconut flour
- 1 teaspoon baking powder
- 4 tablespoon butter
- ½ teaspoon salt
- 1 tablespoon dried dill
- 1 oz Parmesan, grated

Directions:

Wash and trim zucchini. With the help of potato peeler slice zucchini into strips. In the food processor mix up together baking powder, coconut flour, and butter. Add salt and mix up the mixture until you get a dough ball. Roll up the dough ball in the shape of a circle. Transfer the dough in the springform pan. Then make the layer of zucchini over the dough. Spread it with ricotta. Repeat the steps until you use all the ingredients. Sprinkle the last layer of the tart with grated cheese. Preheat oven to 350F and put tart inside. Cook it for 25 minutes. Chill the tart before serving.

Nutrition value/serving: calories 171, fat 10.5, fiber 6.3, carbs 13.1, protein 7.1

Pierogi

Prep time: 15 minutes | *Cooking time:* 5 minutes | *Servings:* 4

Ingredients:

- 1 egg yolk
- 1 cup almond flour
- 2 oz Cheddar cheese, shredded
- 1 teaspoon butter, softened
- 7 oz cauliflower puree with cheese
- 1 teaspoon olive oil

Directions:

Make the dough: mix up together almond flour, egg yolk, and shredded cheese. Stir the mixture until homogenous and microwave for 20 seconds. Then add butter and knead the soft dough. Roll up the dough and cut into triangles. Fill the triangles with cauliflower puree and secure the edges. Preheat skillet well and add olive oil. Place pierogi in the skillet and roast them for 1-2 minutes over the medium heat. Cooked pierogi should have a light golden color.

Nutrition value/serving: calories 200, fat 4.2, fiber 1.7, carbs 4.2, protein 15.1

Creamed Leek

Prep time: 5 minutes | Cooking time: 10 minutes | Servings: 5

Ingredients:

- ½ cup cream cheese
- 8 oz leek, chopped
- 1 teaspoon butter
- 1 teaspoon ground black pepper
- ½ teaspoon smoked paprika

Directions:

Toss butter in the frying pan and melt it. Add chopped leek and sprinkle it with ground black pepper and smoked paprika. Cook the vegetables for 5 minutes over the medium-low heat. After this, add cream cheese and stir until homogenous. Close the lid and cook leek for 5 minutes more.

Nutrition value/serving: calories 117, fat 9, fiber 1, carbs 7.4, protein 2.5

Mint Fritters

Prep time: 10 minutes | Cooking time: 3 minutes | Servings: 2

Ingredients:

- 1 egg, beaten
- 1 tablespoon almond flour
- 1 teaspoon dried mint
- 1 teaspoon dried dill
- 1 zucchini, grated
- ½ teaspoon salt
- 1 tablespoon olive oil

Directions:

In the mixing bowl combine together grated zucchini, salt, dried dill, dried mint, and almond flour. Add beaten egg and mix up the mixture until smooth. Preheat the skillet well and add olive oil. Make the medium fritters from the zucchini mixture. Use two spoons for this step. Place the fritters in the skillet and roast for 1.5 minutes from each side over the medium heat.

Nutrition value/serving: calories 189, fat 16.4, fiber 2.7, carbs 6.8, protein 7.1

Tikka Masala

Prep time: 10 minutes | *Cooking time:* 35 minutes | *Servings:* 4

Ingredients:

- 1-pound cauliflower head
- 1 teaspoon salt
- 2 teaspoon garam masala
- ½ teaspoon ground cumin
- ½ cup heavy cream

- 1 teaspoon cayenne pepper
- ½ teaspoon ground coriander
- 1 teaspoon ground paprika
- ½ teaspoon minced ginger
- 1 tablespoon butter

Directions:

Preheat the oven to 365F. Then line the tray with foil. Cut the cauliflower into florets and place on the tray. Sprinkle vegetables with salt and 1 teaspoon garam masala. Cook the cauliflower florets in the oven for 25 minutes. Meanwhile, toss the butter in the saucepan and melt it. Add remaining garam masala, ground cumin, cayenne pepper, ground paprika, and minced ginger. Simmer the mixture for 5 minutes. Then add baked cauliflower florets and stir well. Cook the meal for 5 minutes more.

Nutrition value/serving: calories 110, fat 8.8, fiber 3.2, carbs 7.3, protein 2.8

Lasagna

Prep time: 15 minutes | *Cooking time:* 30 minutes | *Servings:* 7

Ingredients:

- 2 large eggplants, trimmed
- ½ cup marinara sauce
- 1 cup spinach, chopped
- 1 tablespoon olive oil
- 1 teaspoon salt

- ½ teaspoon ground black pepper
- 5 oz Parmesan, grated
- 5 oz Mozzarella, sliced
- 3 eggs, beaten
- 1 teaspoon butter

Directions:

Slice the eggplants lengthwise and rub with salt, ground black pepper, and olive oil. Place the eggplant slices in the tray and cook in the preheated to 350F oven for 10 minutes. Whisk the eggs and make crepes from the mixture in the non-stick skillet. Remove the eggplants from the oven. Grease the lasagna mold with the butter generously. Make the first layer of eggplants in the mold. Add 1 egg crepe. Then spread it with marinara sauce. Sprinkle with spinach and Parmesan. Repeat the steps until you use all the ingredients. Top lasagna with sliced Mozzarella. Cook the meal in the preheated to 350F oven for 20 minutes.

Nutrition value/serving: calories 227, fat 13.1, fiber 6.1, carbs 13.5, protein 16.6

Casserole

Prep time: 10 minutes | *Cooking time:* 30 minutes | *Servings:* 4

Ingredients:
- 1 cup broccoli
- 1 cup bok choy, chopped
- 7 oz Cheddar, shredded
- 2 tablespoons marinara sauce
- 1 teaspoon butter
- 1 tablespoon cilantro, chopped
- 1 cup heavy cream

Directions:

Grease glass pan with butter. Then place the layer of broccoli. Sprinkle it with cheese little. Add the layer of bok choy and sprinkle it with little cheese again. Add marinara sauce and cilantro. Top the casserole with the remaining cheese and pour heavy cream. Place the meal in the preheated to 355F oven and cook for 30 minutes.

Nutrition value/serving: calories 215, fat 15.9, fiber 1, carbs 4.8, protein 13.8

Quiche

Prep time: 10 minutes | *Cooking time:* 25 minutes | *Servings:* 5

Ingredients:
- 1 cup white mushrooms, chopped
- 1 cup spinach
- 1 cup green beans, boiled
- 1 cup heavy cream
- 8 oz Provolone cheese, shredded
- 5 eggs, beaten

Directions:

Whisk the eggs with the heavy cream. Pour the liquid in the springform pan. Add chopped mushrooms and boiled green beans. After this, chop spinach and add it too. Flatten the mixture with the help of a silicone spatula. Then sprinkle it with shredded Provolone cheese. Preheat the oven to 350F. Transfer the quiche in the oven and cook for 25 minutes. The cooked quiche should have a golden brown surface.

Nutrition value/serving: calories 316, fat 25.4, fiber 1, carbs 4.2, protein 18.6

Nachos

Prep time: 10 minutes | *Cooking time:* 13 minutes | *Servings:* 8

Ingredients:

- 4 bell peppers
- 1 tablespoon olive oil
- ¼ cup olives
- 1 jalapeno pepper, sliced
- 1 teaspoon paprika
- 1 teaspoon chili flakes
- 4 tablespoon almond milk
- 1 teaspoon minced garlic
- 6 oz Cheddar cheese, shredded

Directions:

Cut the bell peppers into halves and remove seeds. Line the tray with foil. Place the bell pepper halves on the foil. Sprinkle the vegetables with olive oil, paprika, chili flakes, and minced garlic. Preheat oven to 365F and put the tray with vegetables inside. Cook the vegetables for 10 minutes. Meanwhile, slice olive and jalapeno pepper. Sprinkle cooked bell peppers with jalapeno, olives, and shredded cheese. Cook the meal for 3 minutes more.

Nutrition value/serving: calories 144, fat 11.2, fiber 1.3, carbs 5.8, protein 6.2

Stuffed Zucchini Pancakes

Prep time: 10 minutes | *Cooking time:* 10 minutes | *Servings:* 2

Ingredients:

- 1 green zucchini, trimmed
- 5 oz Cheddar cheese, shredded
- 1 teaspoon salt
- ½ teaspoon ground black pepper
- ½ teaspoon cayenne pepper
- 1 egg, beaten
- 1 teaspoon olive oil

Directions:

Grate zucchini and squeeze it little to get rid of ½ of all liquid. Transfer the mixture in the mixing bowl. Add salt, ground black pepper, cayenne pepper, and beaten egg. Mix up the mixture until homogenous. Preheat skillet well and pour olive oil inside. Make 4 pancakes from the zucchini mixture and fry them for 1.5 minutes from each side over the medium heat. Then top 2 pancakes with shredded cheese. Cover them with remaining pancakes. Cook the pancakes for 1 minute from each side or until cheese starts to melt.

Nutrition value/serving: calories 350, fat 28.1, fiber 1.3, carbs 3.7, protein 21

Artichoke Peppers

Prep time: 10 *minutes* | *Cooking time:* 15 *minutes* | *Servings:* 2

Ingredients:
- 2 green peppers
- 1 artichoke heart
- 5 oz Parmesan, grated
- 1 teaspoon cayenne pepper
- 2 teaspoon butter

Directions:
Cut the peppers into halves and remove seeds. Chop artichoke heart and mix it up with grated cheese, cayenne pepper, and butter. Fill the peppers with artichoke mixture and wrap in the foil. Preheat the oven to 360F. Put the wrapped peppers in the oven and cook for 15 minutes or until peppers are tender.

Nutrition value/serving: calories 277, fat 17.4, fiber 2.5, carbs 10, protein 24.1

Nut Salad

Prep time: 10 *minutes* | *Servings:* 2

Ingredients:
- ¼ cup walnuts, crushed
- ¼ cup macadamia nuts, crushed
- ¼ cup spinach, chopped
- ¾ cup broccoli florets, boiled
- 1/5 teaspoon onion powder
- 2 tablespoons sour cream

Directions:
In the mixing bowl combine together walnuts, macadamia nuts, and boiled broccoli. For the sauce: churn together sour cream and onion powder. Pour the sauce over salad and stir gently.

Nutrition value/serving: calories 256, fat 24.6, fiber 3.5, carbs 7, protein 6.6

Caprese

Prep time: 10 minutes | *Servings:* 2

Ingredients:

- ½ cup cherry tomatoes
- 4 Mozzarella balls
- 1 tablespoon pesto sauce
- 1 teaspoon olive oil
- ½ cup kalamata olives

Directions:

Mix up together olive oil and pesto sauce. Put all the ingredients in the big bowl and sprinkle with pesto sauce. Shake well until homogenous. Then take skewers and strung the ingredients. Serve the meal or store in the fridge in the closed container up to 2 days.

Nutrition value/serving: calories 340, fat 27.3, fiber 1.8, carbs 4.4, protein 21.4

Eggplant Salad

Prep time: 15 minutes | *Cooking time:* 25 minutes | *Servings:* 6

Ingredients:

- 2 eggplants
- 1 teaspoon salt
- 1 white onion, diced
- 1 teaspoon Pink salt
- 1 oz fresh cilantro
- 3 tablespoon lemon juice
- 4 tablespoon olive oil
- 1 garlic clove, peeled

Directions:

Cut eggplants into halves. Preheat oven to 365F. Put eggplants in the oven and cook for 25 minutes or until they are tender. Meanwhile, blend diced onion and transfer in the cheesecloth. Pour olive oil and lemon juice in the bowl. Squeeze blended onion in the oil mixture. Add salt. Chop cilantro and grind garlic. Add ingredients in the oily mixture too. Stir it. Remove the eggplants from the oven and chill them little. Remove the flesh from the eggplants and transfer in the salad bowl. Add oil mixture and stir gently.

Nutrition value/serving: calories 137, fat 9.8, fiber 7, carbs 13, protein 2.2

Tricolore Salad

Prep time: 10 minutes | Servings: 5

Ingredients:

- 1 avocado, peeled
- ½ cup kalamata olives
- 2 tablespoon olive oil
- 1 teaspoon minced garlic
- ¼ teaspoon salt
- 2 tomatoes, chopped
- 1 teaspoon apple cider vinegar
- 6 oz Provolone cheese, chopped

Directions:

Mix up together salt, apple cider vinegar, minced garlic, and olive oil. Cut kalamata olives into halves. Slice avocado and place in salad bowl. Add olive halves, chopped tomato and cheese. Stir gently and sprinkle with olive oil mixture.

Nutrition value/serving: calories 275, fat 24, fiber 3.7, carbs 7.1, protein 10

"Potato" Salad

Prep time: 10 minutes | Cooking time: 15 minutes | Servings: 4

Ingredients:

- 8 oz turnip, peeled
- 1 carrot, peeled
- 1 bay leaf
- ¼ teaspoon peppercorns
- 1 teaspoon salt
- ½ teaspoon cayenne pepper
- 1 tablespoon fresh parsley, chopped
- 3 eggs, boiled
- 3 tablespoon sour cream
- 1 tablespoon mustard
- 2 cups water, for vegetables

Directions:

Put turnip and carrot in the saucepan. Add water, peppercorns, bay leaf, and salt. Close the lid and boil vegetables for 15 minutes over high heat. The cooked vegetables should be tender. Meanwhile, peel eggs and chop them. Put the chopped eggs in the bowl. Sprinkle them with cayenne pepper and chopped parsley. In the separate bowl stir together mustard and sour cream. When the vegetables are cooked, strain them and transfer in the salad bowl. Add mustard sauce and stir.

Nutrition value/serving: calories 104, fat 6.1, fiber 2, carbs 7.2, protein 5.9

Florentine

Prep time: *10 minutes* | *Cooking time:* *15 minutes* | *Servings: 4*

Ingredients:

- 1 teaspoon butter
- 4 eggs
- 8 oz Edam cheese, shredded
- 1 teaspoon ground paprika
- ¼ teaspoon cayenne pepper
- 2 tablespoon cream cheese

Directions:

Preheat oven to 360F. Preheat the springform pan in the oven. Then grease it with butter. Beat the eggs in the greased pan and sprinkle with cayenne pepper. Top eggs with shredded cheese and spread with cream cheese. Sprinkle the meal with ground paprika. Put it in the oven and cook for 15 minutes or until cheese is light brown at 355F.

Nutrition value/serving: calories 293, fat 22.9, fiber 0.2, carbs 1.6, protein 20.2

Rutabaga Wedges

Prep time: *10 minutes* | *Cooking time: 20 minutes* | *Servings: 4*

Ingredients:

- 2 rutabaga, peeled
- 1 tablespoon lemon juice
- 1 tablespoon olive oil
- ½ teaspoon salt

Directions:

Cut rutabaga into wedges and sprinkle with lemon juice, olive oil, and salt. Stir the vegetables until all the wedges will be in spices. Preheat oven to 360F. Line the tray with baking paper and place wedges in one layer. Transfer the tray in the oven and cook for 20 minutes or until vegetables are light brown.

Nutrition value/serving: calories 100, fat 3.9, fiber 5.6, carbs 15.3, protein 2.4

Fried Eggplants

Prep time: 8 minutes | Cooking time: 17 minutes | Servings: 3

Ingredients:
- 1 large eggplant
- 1 teaspoon minced garlic
- 3 oz Parmesan, grated
- 1 teaspoon dried basil
- 1 teaspoon olive oil

Directions:
Wash and trim eggplants. After this, slice them. Mix up together minced garlic, dried basil, and olive oil. Place the sliced eggplants in the tray in one layer. Spread the vegetables with minced garlic mixture and sprinkle with Parmesan. Transfer the tray in the preheated to 350F oven and cook for 17 minutes or until eggplants are tender.

Nutrition value/serving: calories 144, fat 7.9, fiber 5.4, carbs 10.3, protein 10.7

Crunchy Asparagus Sticks

Prep time: 10 minutes | Cooking time: 10 minutes | Servings: 4

Ingredients:
- 10 oz asparagus, trimmed
- 2 eggs, whisked
- 1 teaspoon ground black pepper
- 1 tablespoon avocado oil
- ½ teaspoon salt

Directions:
Mix up together whisked eggs, ground black pepper, and salt. Preheat avocado oil in the skillet. Dip asparagus into the egg mixture. Then place vegetables in the skillet and roast them from each side until you get a crunchy crust.

Nutrition value/serving: calories 52, fat 2.7, fiber 1.8, carbs 3.5, protein 4.4

Caesar

Prep time: 10 minutes | Servings: 4

Ingredients:

- 1 cup lettuce, chopped
- 1 tablespoon hemp seeds
- 1 teaspoon flax seeds
- 1 tablespoon avocado oil
- 1 avocado, chopped
- 1 oz kalamata olives, chopped
- 2 tablespoons canola oil

Directions:

Put lettuce, hemp seeds, flax seeds, avocado, and olives in the salad bowl. Stir the salad gently. Add avocado oil and canola oil.

Nutrition value/serving: calories 229, fat 23, fiber 4 carbs 5.6, protein 2.4

Almond Cheese

Prep time: 8 hours | Cooking time: 35 minutes | Servings: 6

Ingredients:

- 2 cups almonds, peeled, soaked
- 1 teaspoon salt
- 2 tablespoon lemon juice
- 8 tablespoon water
- 1 teaspoon olive oil

Directions:

Place almonds, salt, lemon juice, and water in the blender. Blend until smooth and transfer into cheesecloth. Squeeze well and leave for 7 hours. Then preheat oven to 385F. Remove the cheesecloth from the almond cheese and brush it with olive oil gently. Place the cheese in the oven and cook for 35 minutes or until you get a golden brown crust. Chill the cheese till the room temperature and only them slice it.

Nutrition value/serving: calories 191, fat 16.7, fiber 4, carbs 6.9, protein 6.7

Cabbage Fritters

Prep time: 15 minutes | Cooking time: 10 minutes | Servings: 6

Ingredients:

- 1-pound white cabbage, shredded
- 1 teaspoon chives, chopped
- 2 eggs, beaten
- 1 tablespoon almond flour
- ½ carrot, peeled, grated
- 1 teaspoon onion powder
- 1 tablespoon coconut butter

Directions:

Place shredded cabbage in the food processor. Add chives, almond flour, eggs, carrot, and onion powder. Blend the mixture until smooth. Make the small fritters from the cabbage mixture. Toss coconut butter in the skillet and melt it. Put the fritters in the skillet and cook for 3 minutes from each side on the medium heat.

Nutrition value/serving: calories 88, fat 5.6, fiber 3, carbs 7, protein 4.1

Desserts

Vegan Chocolate Bars
Prep time: 5 minutes | Cooking time: 1 hour | Servings: 3

Ingredients:
- 3 tablespoon coconut oil
- 3 tablespoon cocoa powder
- 1 tablespoon Erythritol

Directions:
Melt the coconut oil till it is liquid. Then mix up together coconut oil with Erythritol. Stir until homogenous and add cocoa powder. Take the hand whisker and whisk the mixture until smooth. Place the coconut oil mixture into the silicone mold and flatten well. Place it in the freezer for 5 minutes. After this, remove the mold from the freezer and cut it into the bars with the help of the knife. Return the dessert back in the freezer for 1 hour. Store the dessert in the freezer.

Nutrition value/serving: calories 129, fat 14.3, fiber 1.6, carbs 8, protein 1

Brown Fat Bombs
Prep time: 7 minutes | Cooking time: 30 minutes | Servings: 2

Ingredients:
- 1 teaspoon vanilla extract
- 1/3 teaspoon instant coffee
- 1 tablespoon liquid stevia
- 2 tablespoon cocoa powder
- ¾ teaspoon salt
- 1/3 cup coconut butter

Directions:
Take the mixing bowl and combine together vanilla extract, liquid stevia, and instant coffee. Add salt and melted butter. After this, add cocoa powder and mix up the ingredients until you get a soft and smooth texture. Transfer the mixture into the ice cube molds and flatten the surface gently. Place the ice cube molds in the freezer and let them stay there for 30 minutes.

Nutrition value/serving: calories 266, fat 24.7, fiber 8.3, carbs 12.6, protein 3.7

Nut Fudge

Prep time: 8 minutes | Cooking time: 1.5 hours | Servings: 3

Ingredients:
- 1 tablespoon almonds, crushed
- 4 tablespoon almond butter
- ½ teaspoon vanilla extract
- 1 tablespoon Erythritol

Directions:
Take the mixing bowl and combine in it the almond butter, vanilla extract, and Erythritol. Transfer the bowl on the water bath, start to preheat it, and stir gently. When the mixture is homogenous – add crushed almonds, stir it, and remove from the water bath. Place the butter mixture in the mini muffin molds and transfer in the freezer. Freeze it for 1.5 hours.

Nutrition value/serving: calories 144, fat 13, fiber 2.4, carbs 9.5, protein 5

Mug Cake

Prep time: 8 minutes | Cooking time: 1.5 hours | Servings: 4

Ingredients:
- 4 tablespoons pecans, chopped
- 4 teaspoon of cocoa powder
- 4 tablespoon almond flour
- 1 teaspoon vanilla extract
- ½ teaspoon baking powder
- 4 tablespoon almond milk
- 4 teaspoon Erythritol

Directions:
In the mixing bowl mix up together cocoa powder, almond flour, vanilla extract, baking powder, almond milk, and Erythritol. When the mixture is smooth – add chopped pecans. Stir it. Transfer the batter in the mugs and place in the oven. Cook the mug cakes for 10 minutes on 360F. Eat the cakes directly from the mugs.

Nutrition value/serving: calories 91, fat 8.3, fiber 1.8, carbs 3.8, protein 2.1

Cocoa Ice Cream

Prep time: 10 minutes | Cooking time: 30 minutes | Servings: 2

Ingredients:
- 1 can coconut milk
- 1 teaspoon of cocoa powder
- 1 tablespoon Erythritol
- ½ teaspoon vanilla extract

Directions:

Mix up together the coconut milk, cocoa powder, and Erythritol. Add vanilla extract and stir until smooth. Place the coconut mixture in the ice cube molds and place in the freezer for 30 minutes. Then transfer the frozen coconut milk mixture in the blender and blend until smooth. When you get smooth and solid ice cream mixture – it is cooked.

Nutrition value/serving: calories 281, fat 28.7, fiber 2.9, carbs 7.3, protein 2.9

Almond Fat Bombs

Prep time: 10 minutes | Cooking time: 25 minutes | Servings: 7

Ingredients:
- 1 cup almond flour
- 2 tablespoon Erythritol
- 1 teaspoon vanilla extract
- ¼ cup coconut butter
- 1 tablespoon almonds, crushed

Directions:

In the mixing bowl combine together almond flour and crushed almonds. Add Erythritol, vanilla extract, and coconut butter. Use the fork and knead the smooth and soft dough. Add more coconut butter if desired. After this, make the medium size balls with the help of the fingertips and place them in the fridge for at least 25 minutes. When the fat bombs are solid – they are cooked. Store the dessert in the fridge up to 5 days.

Nutrition value/serving: calories 156, fat 13.2, fiber 3.3, carbs 10, protein 4.2

Brownies

Prep time: 10 minutes | *Cooking time:* 15 minutes | *Servings:* 16

Ingredients:
- 1 cup almond milk yogurt
- ½ teaspoon baking powder
- 4 tablespoon cocoa powder
- 1 teaspoon vanilla extract
- 2 cups almond flour
- ½ cup Erythritol
- ¾ teaspoon salt
- 1 tablespoon flax meal

Directions:
Preheat the oven to 355F. In the mixing bowl combine together all the dry ingredients. Then add almond milk yogurt and stir the mixture until you get the batter. Line the tray with the baking paper and transfer batter on it. Flatten brownie batter with the help of a spatula. Place the brownie in the preheated oven and cook for 15 minutes. Then remove the tray with a brownie from the oven. Cut the brownie into 16 serving bars. Transfer the brownie bars in the fridge for 6 hours.

Nutrition value/serving: calories 100, fat 7.8, fiber 2, carbs 10, protein 3.7

Cheesecake

Prep time: 30 minutes | *Cooking time:* 35 minutes | *Servings:* 12

Ingredients:
- ½ cup almond flour
- 3 tablespoon coconut butter
- 1 oz pecans, chopped
- 10 oz Tofutti
- ½ cup almond yogurt
- 4 tablespoon Erythritol
- 3 tablespoons flax meal
- 1 cup water, for cooking

Directions:
Make the pie crust: mix up together almond flour, coconut butter, and chopped pecans. When you get the smooth mixture – transfer it in the springform pan and press well to get the shape of piecrust. Preheat the oven to 360F and place the springform pan with piecrust inside. Cook the piecrust for 4 minutes. Then chill it. After this, in the blender combine together Tofutti, almond yogurt, Erythritol, and flax meal. Blend the mixture until smooth. Transfer the cheesecake mixture over the pie crust and flatten gently. Pour water in the tray and place the springform pan over the water. Transfer the tray in the oven and cook on 355F for 35 minutes. Do not open the oven while cooking. Chill the cooked cheesecake for 25 minutes in the fridge. For better taste leave the cheesecake in the fridge for 7 hours before serving.

Nutrition value/serving: calories 132, fat 11.3, fiber 2, carbs 10.2, protein 2.9

Chocolate Shots

Prep time: 5 minutes | Cooking time: 8 minutes | Servings: 6

Ingredients:

- 2 teaspoon of cocoa powder
- 2 tablespoon Erythritol
- 1 cup coconut milk, creamed
- 2 tablespoon almond milk
- 1 tablespoon coconut flakes

Directions:

Transfer the coconut milk and almond milk in the blender. Blend the mixture until fluffy. After this, add cocoa powder, Erythritol, and whisk it until homogenous. Place the mixture into the pastry bag. Pipe the mixture out in the shots and sprinkle with coconut flakes.

Nutrition value/serving: calories 108, fat 10.9, fiber 1.3, carbs 7.9, protein 1.2

Macaroons

Prep time: 15 minutes | Cooking time: 15 minutes | Servings: 6

Ingredients:

- 1 cup coconut shred
- ½ cup almond flour
- 1/3 cup aquafaba
- 2 teaspoon Erythritol
- 1 oz dark chocolate
- ½ teaspoon vanilla extract

Directions:

Line the tray with the baking paper and place coconut shred over it. Flatten it. Preheat the oven to 360 F and put the tray with the coconut shred inside it. Toast it for 2-3 minutes. After this, combine together toasted coconut shred, almond flour, vanilla extract, and Erythritol. Stir the mixture. Pour aquafaba into a separate bowl and whisk it with the help of mixer until you get soft peaks. Combine together aquafaba and dry ingredients. Mix up the mixture well. Scoop the mixture and make medium balls. Place the balls in the tray and press them gently with the help of the hand palm. Cook the macaroons for 15 minutes. Meanwhile, melt the dark chocolate. When the macaroons are cooked – chill them till the room temperature and dip ½ part of every macaroon in the chocolate.

Nutrition value/serving: calories 171, fat 14.7, fiber 2.9, carbs 10.1, protein 3.3

Zucchini Bars

Prep time: 10 minutes | *Cooking time:* 15 minutes | *Servings:* 10

Ingredients:

- 1 zucchini, shredded
- 1 cup almond flour
- ¼ cup coconut butter
- ½ teaspoon baking powder
- 1 teaspoon lemon juice
- 1/3 cup Erythritol
- 1 teaspoon vanilla extract

Directions:

In the mixing bowl combine together shredded zucchini, almond flour, baking powder, lemon juice, and Erythritol. Stir gently and add coconut butter and vanilla extract. Mix up the mixture with the help of the spoon and place it in the lined with the parchment baking tray. Flatten the mixture and cook it on 365F for 15 minutes. After this, remove the zucchini dessert from the oven and cut it into the bars with the help of a pizza knife.

Nutrition value/serving: calories 58, fat 5, fiber 2.5, carbs 10.4, protein 1.2

Coconut Cookies

Prep time: 10 minutes | *Cooking time:* 10 minutes | *Servings:* 12

Ingredients:

- 1 cup coconut flour
- ½ cup coconut shred
- 2 egg whites
- 3 tablespoon Erythritol
- 1 tablespoon coconut oil

Directions:

Whisk the eggs whites until you get soft peaks. Combine together whisked egg whites, coconut shred, coconut flour, and Erythritol. Stir gently and add coconut oil. Mix up the mixture until homogenous. Make the small size cooked from the coconut mixture and press them gently. Line the baking tray with the baking paper. Place the cookies on the tray and cook them at 365F for 10 minutes. Check the cookies after 5 minutes of cooking. When the cookies are cooked – chill them till the room temperature and store in the closed glass jar.

Nutrition value/serving: calories 75, fat 4.4, fiber 4.4, carbs 11.3, protein 2.2

Red Velvet Muffins

Prep time: 10 minutes | Cooking time: 10 minutes | Servings: 6

Ingredients:

- 3 tablespoon almond butter
- ¼ cup almond milk
- 1 teaspoon vanilla extract
- ½ teaspoon baking powder
- 1 cup almond flour
- 1 teaspoon red food coloring

Directions:

Melt the almond butter and combine it together with the vanilla extract and food coloring. When the mixture is smooth – add baking powder, almond milk, and almond flour. Make the homogenous batter. Preheat the oven to 360F. Fill ½ part of every muffin mold with the red batter. Transfer the molds in the oven and cook for 10 minutes. Check the muffins with the help of the toothpick and cook them for 2-3 minutes more if need.

Nutrition value/serving: calories 186, fat 15.8, fiber 3, carbs 6.3, protein 5.9

Gingerbread Muffins

Prep time: 8 minutes | Cooking time: 11 minutes | Servings: 10

Ingredients:

- 1 cup coconut flour
- 1 cup almond flour
- 1/2 cup heavy cream
- 4 tablespoon Erythritol
- 1 teaspoon vanilla extract
- 1 teaspoon ground ginger
- 1/2 teaspoon ground cinnamon
- 1/2 teaspoon ground cloves

Directions:

Mix up together all the ingredients in the mixing bowl. Use the hand mixer to make the mixture smooth and homogenous. After this, fill ½ part of every muffin mold with the smooth batter. Cook the muffins at 365F for 11 minutes. When the time is over – chill the muffins till the room temperature.

Nutrition value/serving: calories 45, fat 3.9, fiber 0.9, carbs 7.9, protein 1

Eggnog

Prep time: 8 minutes | Cooking time: 11 minutes | Servings: 4

Ingredients:

- 1 cup almond milk
- 6 oz pecans, chopped
- 2 tablespoon protein powder
- 2 teaspoon Erythritol
- ½ teaspoon ground cinnamon
- ¾ teaspoon ground nutmeg

Directions:

Put all the ingredients in the food processor and blend until smooth. Pour Eggnog into the serving small glasses. Better to serve the dessert chilled.

Nutrition value/serving: calories 467, fat 45.3, fiber 6.1, carbs 13.2, protein 11.5

Chocolate Pumpkins

Prep time: 15 minutes | Cooking time: 4 minutes | Servings: 4

Ingredients:

- 1 cup almond flour
- 1 tablespoon pumpkin puree
- 2 teaspoon liquid stevia
- 1 teaspoon vanilla extract
- 1 oz sugar-free dark chocolate
- 1 tablespoon cocoa butter

Directions:

Mix up together almond flour, pumpkin puree, liquid stevia, and vanilla extract. Knead the smooth dough. Make the medium size balls from the dough. Then make the shape of pumpkins from the balls. Use the fingertips for this step. Place the "pumpkins" on the tray. Cook the dessert for 4 minutes at 365F. Meanwhile, melt together cocoa butter and dark chocolate. Chill the cooked "pumpkins" and dip into the melted chocolate mixture. Transfer the dessert in the fridge and let it there until firm.

Nutrition value/serving: calories 238, fat 19.5, fiber 3.8, carbs 10.9, protein 6.4

Almond Cupcakes

Prep time: 10 minutes | Cooking time: 15 minutes | Servings: 5

Ingredients:
- 3 tablespoon almond butter
- 4 tablespoon almond milk
- 1 tablespoon Erythritol
- 3 tablespoon flax meal
- ½ teaspoon instant coffee
- 1/3 teaspoon baking powder
- ½ cup coconut milk, creamed

Directions:
Stir the instant coffee in the almond milk. Add almond butter and flax meal. After this, add baking powder and Erythritol. Stir the mass until smooth. Preheat the oven to 365F. Fill 1/3 part of every cupcake mold with the coffee mixture. Put the cupcakes in the oven and cook for 15 minutes or until the cupcakes are firmed. Meanwhile, whip the coconut milk until fluffy. Chill the cooked cupcakes well and decorate with the coconut milk frosting.

Nutrition value/serving: calories 180, fat 14.6, fiber 2.7, carbs 10.9, protein 4.3

Dulce De Leche

Prep time: 10 minutes | Cooking time: 25 minutes | Servings: 4

Ingredients:
- 1 can creamed coconut milk
- 4 tablespoon swerve
- 1 tablespoon Erythritol
- 1 teaspoon vanilla extract

Directions:
In the saucepan mix up together coconut milk, swerve, Erythritol, and vanilla extract. Stir gently. Put the saucepan on the high heat and stir constantly. Reduce the heat till medium-low when the liquid starts to boil. Cook the dessert for 20 minutes. Stir it constantly. Transfer cooked Dulce de leche in the glass jar and chill for 2-3 hours in the fridge.

Nutrition value/serving: calories 33, fat 0, fiber 0.3, carbs 8.7, protein 0.5

Carrot Cakes

Prep time: 10 minutes | Cooking time: 7 minutes | Servings: 6

Ingredients:
- 5 tablespoon almond flour
- 5 tablespoon butter, softened
- 1 tablespoon carrot, grated
- 5 teaspoon liquid stevia
- ½ teaspoon vanilla extract

Directions:

In the mixing bowl combine together softened butter, almond flour, and liquid stevia. Add vanilla extract and grated carrot. Stir the mixture with the help of the fork. Take the silicone small molds and spread the dough evenly inside the molds. Preheat the oven to 365F. Put the cakes in the oven and cook for 7 minutes. Remove the cooked carrot cakes from the oven and chill them well. After some time the cakes become firm.

Nutrition value/serving: calories 137, fat 14.2, fiber 0.6, carbs 1.4, protein 1.3

Chocolate Pie

Prep time: 10 minutes | Cooking time: 25 minutes | Servings: 14

Ingredients:
- 1 cup almond flour
- ½ cup flax meal
- ½ cup Erythritol
- 5 eggs, beaten
- 1 teaspoon vanilla extract
- ½ teaspoon ground nutmeg
- ¼ cup almond milk
- 1 tablespoon cocoa powder
- 1 teaspoon baking powder
- ½ teaspoon lemon juice
- 1 tablespoon whipped cream

Directions:

In the mixing bowl combine together all dry ingredients. Then add eggs, vanilla extract, almond milk, and lemon juice. Use the hand mixer to mix up the mixture. Line the springform pan with the parchment. Transfer the chocolate batter in the springform pan and flatten gently with the silicone spatula. Put the springform pan in the preheated to 365F oven and cook for 25 minutes. Check if the pie is cooked and remove it from the oven. Chill it and spread with the whipped cream.

Nutrition value/serving: calories 58, fat 4.4, fiber 1.5, carbs 9.2, protein 3.4

Keto Cookies

Prep time: 10 minutes | Cooking time: 10 minutes | Servings: 4

Ingredients:
- 2 tablespoon coconut butter
- ½ cup coconut flakes
- 1 tablespoon butter
- 2 egg yolks
- 1 tablespoon Erythritol
- 2 teaspoon sugar-free dark chocolate

Directions:

Mix up together coconut flakes, coconut butter, egg yolks, and Erythritol. Chop the dark chocolate and add it in the coconut mixture. Preheat the oven to 360F. Line the baking tray with the baking paper. Scoop the coconut mixture in the baking tray to get small size balls. Transfer the baking tray in the oven and cook for 10 minutes. Chill the cookies till the room temperature.

Nutrition value/serving: calories 153, fat 14.3, fiber 2.5, carbs 5.1, protein 2.5

Mousse

Prep time: 10 minutes | Servings: 2

Ingredients:
- ½ cup heavy cream
- 5 scoop stevia
- 1 tablespoon cocoa powder
- 1 teaspoon vanilla extract
- 1 avocado, peeled

Directions:

Put the avocado, heavy cream, cocoa powder, stevia, and vanilla extract in the food processor. Blend the mixture until homogenous and smooth. Pour the cooked mousse in the glasses.

Nutrition value/serving: calories 321, fat 31.1, fiber 7.6, carbs 11.2, protein 3.1

Delicious Sweet Shake

Prep time: *10 minutes* | *Cooking time:* *10 minutes* | *Servings:* 2

Ingredients:

- ½ cup almond milk
- 3 teaspoon almond butter
- ½ teaspoon of cocoa powder
- ¼ teaspoon vanilla extract
- ¼ teaspoon ground cinnamon
- 1 teaspoon hemp seeds
- 1 tablespoon chia seeds
- 1 tablespoon Erythritol

Directions:

Put all the ingredients in the blender and blend until smooth. Pour the cooked shake in the serving glasses.

Nutrition value/serving: calories 207, fat 16.9, fiber 5.2, carbs 10.1, protein 7

Avocado Pops

Prep time: *10 minutes* | *Servings:* 2

Ingredients:

- 1 avocado
- 2 tablespoon swerve
- ¼ cup almond milk
- ½ teaspoon vanilla extract

Directions:

Peel the avocado and chop it roughly. Put the chopped avocado in the blender. Add almond milk, swerve, and vanilla extract. Blend the mixture well. Pour the mixture into the popsicle molds and freeze well.

Nutrition value/serving: calories 282, fat 26.8, fiber 7.4, carbs 12.4, protein 2.6

Caramel

*Prep time: 5 minutes | **Cooking time:** 10 minutes | **Servings:** 2*

Ingredients:
- ¼ cup heavy cream
- 5 tablespoon swerve
- 2 tablespoon butter
- ½ teaspoon vanilla extract

Directions:

Melt butter in the saucepan. Add swerve and stir it well. Cook the mixture for 4 minutes over the medium heat. Stir it from time to time. Then add vanilla extract and heavy cream. Stir the caramel and simmer it for 5 minutes over the medium heat. When the caramel gest light golden color, it is cooked.

Nutrition value/serving: calories 169, fat 17.1, fiber 0, carbs 5.6, protein 0.4

Conclusion

This book proves that following the vegetarian lifestyle and Keto diet is possible but not easy much. On the last page of this cookbook, you will find valuable pieces of advice about products that are most useful for your vegetarian Keto diet. As you have already understood the main products for Keto vegans are dairy products and eggs. They are high in fat and can give you 25% percent of calories per day. What are the main products that are high in proteins and vegan-friendly? These are tofu, seitan, and tempeh. Each of these ingredients is low in carbs. The list of food you can eat while Vegetarian Keto diet contains leafy greens such as spinach or Italian dark leaf kale; ground vegetables (cauliflower, broccoli, zucchini); pistachios, sunflower seeds, macadamia nuts, walnuts, almonds, pumpkin seeds, etc.; avocado, blueberries, blackberries, and strawberries. If we talk about desserts, the best keto sweeteners are Truvia, stevia, and Erythritol. During cooking, you can also use coconut and olive oils, macadamia, MCT and avocado oils. Protein powder is one more good options for your vegetarian Keto meal. The best choice is 100% grass-fed whey protein powder. You can easily add it into the handmade milkshakes and smoothies. There is a huge range of alternatives for Keto lovers. For instance, heavy cream can be substituted with coconut cream; butter can be replaced by coconut oil. You can be amazed but even eggs can be avoided by using The Vegg. As you see, following the diet can be easy if you find the right approach for it. The only caution is to not over-diet. Entering the keto diet should be gradual. Since this is a stress for the body and it needs time to adapt to a new way of life.If you feel a deterioration in your health, consult a doctor, correct your daily meal plan, or stop the diet till the time your body will be ready for it.

Recipe Index

Almond
Granola, 10
Yogurt Bowl, 11
Fragrant Smoothie, 13
Baked Asparagus with Eggs, 20
Falafel, 30
Fried Broccoli, 37
Almond Cheese, 59
Nut Fudge, 60
Almond Fat Bombs, 61

Almond flour
Breakfast Pizza, 7
Donuts, 7
Waffles, 8
No at meal, 9
Zucchini Tots, 12
Pancakes, 15
Breakfast Bread, 16
Breakfast Chocolate Balls, 16
Cup Muffin, 18
Zucchini Gratin, 23
Avocado Pie, 28
Falafel, 30
Quesadillas, 31
Fried Cheese, 34
Broccoli Fritters, 41
Enchiladas, 46
Pierogi, 47
Mint Fritters, 48
Cabbage Fritters, 58
Mug Cake, 60
Almond Fat Bombs, 61
Brownies, 62
Cheesecake, 62
Macaroons, 63
Zucchini Bars, 64

Red Velvet Muffins, 65
Gingerbread Muffins, 65
Chocolate Pumpkins, 66
Carrot Cakes, 68
Chocolate Pie, 68

Almond milk
Crepes, 8
No at meal, 9
Chia Pudding, 10
Morning Coffee Shake, 11
Almond Scramble, 14
Pancakes, 15
Breakfast Bread, 16
Coconut Porridge, 19
Cup Muffin, 18
Cauliflower Hash Brown Bowl, 20
Risotto, 22
Kale Soup, 26
Tofu Wraps, 27
Avocado Pie, 28
Egg Salad, 31
Mashed Cauliflower, 33
Zucchini Pasta, 38
Fettuccine, 40
Sauteed Cabbage, 44
Nachos, 51
Mug Cake, 60
Chocolate Shots, 63
Red Velvet Muffins, 65
Eggnog, 68
Almond Cupcakes, 68
Chocolate Pie, 68
Delicious Sweet Shake, 70
Avocado Pops, 70
Almond milk yogurt
Yogurt Bowl, 11

Brownies, 62
Cheesecake, 62

Artichoke
Artichoke Peppers, 52
Garlic Artichokes, 43

Asparagus
Baked Asparagus with Eggs, 20
Crunchy Asparagus Sticks, 56

Avocado
Avocado Eggs, 25
Avocado Pie, 28
Egg Salad, 31
Cabbage Salad, 34
Zucchini Pasta, 38
Enchiladas, 46
Tricolore Salad, 54
Caesar, 57
Mousse, 69
Avocado Pops, 70

Beans
Green Beans Salad, 21
Quiche, 50

Blackberries
Chia Pudding, 10
Yogurt Bowl, 11

Bok choy
Bok Choy Salad, 27
Casserole, 50

Broccoli
Broccoli Fritters, 21
Fried Broccoli, 37

Broccoli Fritters, 41
Casserole, 50
Nut Salad, 52

Brussel sprouts
Brussel Sprouts with Nuts, 37

Cabbage
Cabbage Salad, 34
Roasted Cabbage, 38
Sauteed Cabbage, 44
Cabbage Fritters, 58

Carrot
Turnip Slaw, 43
"Potato" Salad, 54
Cabbage Fritters, 58
Carrot Cakes, 68

Cauliflower
Breakfast Pizza, 7
Cauliflower Hash Brown Bowl, 20
Green Beans Salad, 21
Risotto, 22
Kale Soup, 26
Falafel, 30
Mashed Cauliflower, 33
Fragrant Cauliflower Steaks, 33
Hummus, 35
Curry Rice, 42
Tikka Masala, 49
Pierogi, 47

Celery
Almond Scramble, 14
Keto Casserole, 18
Kale Soup, 26

Avocado Pie, 28

Chard
Swiss Chard, 45

Cheddar
Zucchini Gratin, 23
Eggplant Gratin, 24
Turnip Gratin, 28
Eggplant Pizza, 30
Quesadillas, 31
Enchiladas, 46
Pierogi, 47
Casserole, 50
Nachos, 51
Stuffed Zucchini Pancakes, 51

Chia seeds
No at meal, 9
Chia Pudding, 10
Granola, 10
Coconut Porridge, 17
Delicious Sweet Shake, 70

Chili
Herbed Eggs, 9
Almond Scramble, 14
Broccoli Fritters, 21
Spinach Soup, 29
Mashed Cauliflower, 33
Nachos, 51
Dill Mushroom Hats, 17
Bok Choy Salad, 27

Chocolate
Breakfast Chocolate Balls, 16
Macaroons, 63
Chocolate Pumpkins, 66
Keto Cookies, 69

Cocoa butter
Vanilla Sticks, 14

Cocoa powder
Vegan Chocolate Bars, 59
Brown Fat Bombs, 59
Mug Cake, 60
Cocoa Ice Cream, 61
Chocolate Shots, 63
Chocolate Shots, 63
Chocolate Pie, 68
Mousse, 69
Delicious Sweet Shake, 70

Coconut flour
Crepes, 8
Breakfast Bagels, 13
Zucchini Tart, 47
Coconut Cookies, 64
Gingerbread Muffins, 65

Coconut milk
Fragrant Smoothie, 14
Shirataki Noodles, 38
Dill Radish, 42
Enchiladas, 46
Cocoa Ice Cream, 61
Almond Cupcakes, 67
Dulce De Leche, 67

Coconut shred
No at meal, 9
Granola, 10
Yogurt Bowl, 11
Coconut Porridge, 17
Cup Muffin, 18

Macaroons, 63
Coconut Cookies, 64

Coffee
Morning Coffee Shake, 11
Brown Fat Bombs, 59
Almond Cupcakes, 67

Cream cheese
Creamed Leek, 48
Florentine, 55

Eggplant
Eggplant Rolls, 22
Eggplant Gratin, 24
Eggplant Pizza, 30
Low Carb Baked Vegetables, 39
Fried Eggplants, 56
Lasagna, 49
Eggplant Salad, 53

Eggs
Breakfast Pizza, 7
Crepes, 8
Waffles, 8
Herbed Eggs, 9
Keto Casserole, 18
Spinach Muffin, 19
Baked Asparagus with Eggs, 20
Broccoli Fritters, 21
Avocado Eggs, 25
Spinach Pie, 26
Egg Salad, 31
Quesadillas, 31
Deviled Eggs, 36
Lasagna, 49
Quiche, 50
"Potato" Salad, 54

Florentine, 55
Crunchy Asparagus Sticks, 56
Cabbage Fritters, 58
Chocolate Pie, 68

Goat cheese
Zucchini Boats, 23
Fried Cheese, 34

Halloumi cheese
Roasted Halloumi, 35

Heavy cream
Waffles, 8
Breakfast Chocolate Balls, 16
Zucchini Gratin, 23
Eggplant Gratin, 24
Turnip Gratin, 28
Spinach in Cream, 41
Tikka Masala, 49
Casserole, 50
Mousse, 69
Caramel, 71

Jicama
French Fries, 40

Kale
Kale Soup, 26

Leek
Creamed Leek, 48

Lettuce
Green Beans Salad, 21
Caesar, 57

Macadamia nuts

Granola, 10
Sauteed Cabbage, 44
Nut Salad, 52

Mozzarella
Eggplant Rolls, 22
Gnocchi, 29
Lasagna, 49
Caprese, 53

Mushrooms
Green Frittata, 15
Dill Mushroom Hats, 17
Cauliflower Hash Brown Bowl, 20
Risotto, 22
Tofu Wraps, 27
Low Carb Baked Vegetables, 39
Quiche, 50
Portobello Mushrooms, 25

Olives
Eggplant Salad, 53
Tricolore Salad, 54
Caesar, 57

Parmesan
Breakfast Pizza, 7
Keto Casserole, 18
Broccoli Fritters, 21
Eggplant Gratin, 24
Spinach Pie, 26
Fragrant Cauliflower Steaks, 33
Zucchini Tart, 47
Lasagna, 49
Artichoke Peppers, 52
Fried Eggplants, 56

Pecans

Coconut Porridge, 17
Brussel Sprouts with Nuts, 37
Mug Cake, 60
Cheesecake, 62
Eggnog, 66

Pepper
Enchiladas, 46
Low Carb Baked Vegetables, 39
Nachos, 51
Artichoke Peppers, 52

Provolone cheese
Cheese Rolls, 32
Spinach in Cream, 41
Quiche, 50

Pumpkin
Pancakes, 15
Chocolate Pumpkins, 66

Radish
Dill Radish, 42

Raspberries
Yogurt Bowl, 11

Ricotta cheese
Zucchini Tart, 47

Rutabaga
Rutabaga Swirls, 39
Spiced Rutabaga, 45
Rutabaga Wedges, 55

Spinach
Breakfast Pizza, 7

Tofu Scramble, 12
Green Frittata, 15
Spinach Muffin, 19
Spinach Pie, 26
Spinach Soup, 29
Quesadillas, 31
Cabbage Salad, 34
Zucchini Pasta, 38
Spinach in Cream, 41
Quiche, 50
Nut Salad, 52

Tahini paste
Breakfast Bagels, 13
Green Frittata, 15
Kale Soup, 26
Falafel, 30
Hummus, 35
Keto Satay, 46

Tofu
Tofu Scramble, 12
Almond Scramble, 14
Vanilla Sticks, 14
Green Frittata, 15
Dill Mushroom Hats, 17
Risotto, 22
Portobello Mushrooms, 25
Tofu Wraps, 27
Bok Choy Salad, 27

Broccoli Fritters, 41
Keto Satay, 46

Tomato
Greek Salad, 24
Eggplant Pizza, 30
Caprese, 53

Turnip
Turnip Gratin, 28
Turnip Slaw, 43
"Potato" Salad, 54

Walnuts
Granola, 10
Nut Salad, 52

Zucchini
Zucchini Tots, 12
Spinach Muffin, 19
Zucchini Gratin, 23
Zucchini Boats, 23
Zucchini Pasta, 38
Fettuccine, 40
Zucchini Tart, 47
Mint Fritters, 48
Stuffed Zucchini Pancakes, 51
Zucchini Bars, 64

Made in the USA
Middletown, DE
04 March 2021